The Architect

This book will help you become the architect of your own destiny

Palewell Press

The Architect

Steve Allen Champion &
Craig Anthony Ross

PP

The Architect

First edition 2019 from Palewell Press, www.palewellpress.co.uk

ISBN 978-1-911587-14-9

The cover design is Copyright © 2019 DeCarlo R Garrett Jr. at Team Garrett Music and Design
The photo of Raymond Lee Washington was downloaded from https://alchetron.com/cdn/

A CIP catalogue record for this title is available from the British Library.

ACKNOWLEDGEMENTS

No book is a solo effort. We could not have completed this work without the loyal support we received from so many while writing it. We owe our deep appreciation to some dedicated people whose assistance and feedback brought this book to fruition. Most of these people entered our lives when we needed them most and we believe that without their invaluable contributions this book would be very different. What follows is but a humble attempt to acknowledge our enormous debt of gratitude.

To our brother Ajamu (Stanley Tookie Williams) whose voice and presence was always with us throughout the writing: we don't forget. Nothing has been left behind.

We thank our good friend Betsy Vriend immensely for typing portions of the original manuscript and starting the long process of editing while giving us clear direction.

We are truly indebted to Regina Scott for her scholarship and providing us with resource materials that were right on time. May the Orishas guide your path always.

We send a big power salute to our sister Jendayi O. Foluke who always sent us positive vibes and the right kind of ammunition to keep us on point. Asante sana, dada.

To our personal Ms. Moneypenny, Bridget Ross, we simply cannot thank you enough. Without your lightning fast fingers, absolute devotion and otherworldly efficiency, the drafts and revisions you worked on would still need doing. You know the meaning of the lotus.

Thank you to Ms. Tiffany Lewis for graciously doing research and providing data indispensable to our work. You helped in countless ways to make the book a reality.

We are also very grateful to our friend, editor, and magician, Professor Tom Kerr, whose critical advice, expertise, and patience helped us bring greater clarity to each chapter and to the work as a whole. Thank you for your enduring commitment, confidence and uncommon generosity on our behalf.

To Nicola White, we profoundly thank you for your encouraging words and for introducing us to our publisher. Your intuition was on point. You have our deepest gratitude.

We can't begin to thank Camilla Reeve, our Editor at Palewell Press, who immediately understood our vision for *The Architect* and made critical suggestions that enriched the text and made it more accessible. Without your belief and valuable input this book wouldn't be published. Thank you for the hundredth time.

To our brother and homeboy DeCarlo in Colorado, much love, for unleashing your creativity in designing the cover of this book. You intuitively understood what we wanted and created something truly memorable in the eleventh hour.

In addition, we would like to thank the many street soldiers we've encountered over the years who have been a constant source of inspiration, encouragement, and resolve. We feel you.

We cannot close without giving our "circle" on the row (you know who you are) a big salute of respect for listening to our sermons about The Architect for years. You guys showed nothing but infinite support, thank you. You brothers are true Architects.

Steve Champion and Craig Ross

In dedication to our brothers, the legacy will be transformed.

Stanley Tookie Williams
1953-2005

Raymond Lee Washington
1953-1979

CONTENTS

PROLOGUE:
WHO THIS BOOK IS FOR

"In the general framework of the daily struggle this battle against ourselves — no matter what difficulties the enemy may create — remains the most difficult of all..." — **Amilcar Cabral**

For Homeboys And Homegirls

Writing this book wasn't easy. We had plenty of challenges and obstacles throughout the process: being isolated in San Quentin's Adjustment Center, having our large personal library reduced to three books, writing every draft longhand, having pages of our manuscript taken or lost in cell searches, and waiting weeks, sometimes months, due to the slow prison mail system, for the feedback and edited pages our editor, Tom Kerr, would send. But with dogged determination we prevailed. We never lost sight of why we were writing: our profound need to awaken the consciousness of gang members and promote self-transformation and social change.

Our book is for gang members, both former and active. We were once active gang members ourselves, so we know and understand the gang life intimately. Our own self-transformation is reflected in this book. But to learn more about that, read "The Sacred Eye of the Falcon."

Personal experience has shown us that everything we speak about is achievable. But it all depends on the willingness and commitment of individuals who heed our call.

Some of the ideas will be challenging for us to explain and you to understand. So we open each section with a personal letter addressed to you, our Homie, saying why we want you to keep reading on.

This book is quite long. It isn't essential for people to read all of it right off. You can take it gradually, one part or section after another, or just dip into sections in the order you find them most interesting. The Appendices and Bibliography at the back offer extra reading for anyone who enjoys exploring new ideas. But whatever parts you read, these are our genuine beliefs, formed during hard personal experiences and self-transformation.

For Those Who Work With Gangs

This book is also for anyone who wants to understand how to help create a new social paradigm through gang transformation. We present a model for gang members to develop a new consciousness of change that can transform their lives and communities in positive and extraordinary ways. People who work with gang members can use any part of our model and develop their own programs and strategies.

Solutions to gang violence will come not from old ideas like gang suppression, prevention, and interventionist strategies.

- Gang Suppression - Law enforcement has used suppression tactics, tougher anti-gang laws, racial profiling, and, often, physical brutality. History shows the cumulative blowback of these police tactics causes gangs to migrate beyond the limits of their neighborhood, city, and state to gain footholds in places that traditionally have had no gang presence.
- Gang prevention groups target "at-risk" kids to prevent them from joining a gang, but they simply don't have the resources to reach all of the kids that need help. Consequently, many young people will become gang members.
- Gang interventionists try to mediate conflicts between gangs, *after* the shots have already been fired, to try to stop further retaliatory actions, but their success or failure is tied to how much the gang members trust and respect them.

3

Over time, we've seen gangs decrease and increase in numbers. There may be a lull in violence as they shift locations and change colors or even get hired as extras in videos and movies, but they will not disappear. Strategies for dealing with them must be realistic, pragmatic, *and* radical.

The problem of gang violence is a chronic illness passed on from one generation to the next. Despite all of the initiatives, strategies and laws used to combat gang violence over the past 30 years, we're no closer to its resolution. We need more than critical dialogue, pre-packaged promises and anti-gang programs. We need a movement, a *transformational* movement that affects gang members, and thus the gangs themselves.

Our idea of a community revolution is not a cure-all for gang violence. No approach could succeed in doing that. Instead, *The Architect* is talking about urban diplomacy. It sets the stage for the cultivation of a new breed of urban leaders.

When people have a vested interest in their neighborhood, they tend to play constructive roles in the community. If we want gang violence to stop, we need to

- Develop transformative leaders within gangs;

- Help gang members become the architects of their own destiny;
- Provide the tools they need to achieve this whether it's a mentor, training, investment, or long-term and short-term organizational support.

Some critics will try to dismiss the idea that gang members can transform their lives. But what about all the men and women who were gang members and are now business professionals, academics, actors, recording artists, activists, motivational speakers, authors, and pastors?

What about Nipsey Hussle? He became the epitome of transformation, of what is possible, when you choose positive change for yourself, your neighborhood and community.

We didn't know Nipsey, but what we did know about him we applaud and respect. He was living exactly what the Architect represents. Because of his vision he was on the precipice of great success; and was a shining example to millions. If his legacy is to have an enduring impact then the accomplishments he achieved must be duplicated over and over again, until it is no longer exceptional, but the norm.

Franklin Greenwald has said, "We cannot change unless we survive, but we will not survive unless we change." This idea is the fulcrum on which we stand today. It conveys the urgency and importance of action.

To *all* gang members we say that what's holding you back is not the judicial system with its systemic problems of racism and corruption that stack the deck against you; not law enforcement that sees you as urban terrorists or vermin; not the revolving doors of the prison industrial complex; not the politics that exclude and disempower you! The only thing really holding you back is yourself, when you choose not to change.

Why Be An Architect?

"As the foundation is laid, so the walls of the house will rise."—**Author unknown**

In the ancient world, Architects were known as "master builders." It was these craftsmen who constructed the great monuments, pyramids, temples and palaces around the world. According to ancient mystery teachings, the title of "master builder" was only given to someone who had undergone rigorous training and transformation.

Thus, Architects were not merely concerned with the construction of edifices, but also with the symbolic temple—the Self.

The supreme ambition of every Architect is to build his or her character and intellect to a level of illumination from which the best of his or her potential can flow. In doing this, the Architect functions from a moral, ethical and spiritual foundation that is the compass of his or her life.

The philosophy of the Architect is very simple: right thinking leads to right action.

Architects always strive for unity, betterment, and progress. They live every day conscious of their commitment, responsibility, and purpose.

To become an Architect is to live in a manner that honors a commitment to positive change, personal growth, and that inspires others to work towards transforming themselves, their communities, and the world.

Creed Of The Architect

- **I BELIEVE** the actions of an Architect are founded on ideas that will ensure growth, development, and progress in all areas of life.

- **I BELIEVE** collectivity must always be placed ahead of personal agendas and self-interest.
- **I BELIEVE** in equality of and respect for all men and women.
- **I BELIEVE** an Architect must be willing to make sacrifices for change and progress.
- **I BELIEVE** an Architect must promote knowledge, education, vocation, public service, and correctly guide those who choose the path of the Architect.
- **I BELIEVE** every Architect must take a stand against chaos and promote progress, peace and individual responsibility.

Our Message, Your Challenge

"There's nothing more powerful than an idea whose time has come." —Victor Hugo

Let us be brutally honest. Crips, Bloods and other cliques have fanatically submitted their lives, neighborhoods and families to a long cycle of terror and devastation. Their focus on violence and self-hate has consumed several generations of young men and women.

How many more young people must be buried or incarcerated before it all ends? How many more mothers must lose a child before we find the solution? How many more children must be left to raise themselves before we come up with answers that make sense?

I believe we all want the streets safe enough for kids to play and people to walk without fear of being a victim. But with gang members submerged in an absolutism that perpetuates horrific violence, this isn't the case.

We need to stop waiting for other people or agencies to solve the problems of urban poor communities. Government programs are too under-funded and badly managed to make a serious difference. And no matter how much we pray for divine intervention, God is not going to swoop down from heaven and micromanage our lives.

So we're calling on all of you—street soldiers, young, old, men, women and those incarcerated—to contribute your minds and energy to bringing about a new paradigm in our communities. We challenge you to:

- Replace hatred with wisdom and bloodshed with reconciliation;
- Take a stand against the protracted violence in our collective lives;
- Become the Architects of change and transformation in your neighborhood.

We ask no more of you than what you are willing to give. All you have to do is make the choice and commitment to be a part of the solution.

You may ask: Why should I step up and get involved if the problems never seem to change? Why should I take a stand when others don't?

The answer is you shouldn't change merely to prove a point, but because you understand exactly what's at stake—your future, your life— and because you have come to the realization that if you don't take a stand nothing will change.

So we ask all gang members: Do you want a better life? A different life? If so, are you prepared to acknowledge a contradiction between what you truly want and what you do to get it? Every time you engage in ethnic self-cleansing—killing and brutalizing each other—you openly aid anyone who capitalizes on or profits from the lunacy and the misery you leave in your wake. All those years of death and mayhem without winning so much as a single acre of land, without securing the rights to natural resources, and without gaining power within the political or business world— what the hell were we thinking?

We, the authors of this book, were once hardcore gang members and part of the cycle of destruction. We used to ignore advice of this kind, but we hope you will consider our ideas. If you can change your choices and the thinking that rules your behavior, you will completely change your life for the better.

Don't be a willing slave to chaos; instead, choose to be an Architect of order. Each day you delay only increases the deterioration and destruction of your communities.

The answers to these problems do not lie in the surrender to a fate ruled by statistics that claim you will be on probation or parole by the time you're 21, nor will they come from the psychology of nihilism that engenders the "I don't give a fuck" attitude. The answers *will* be found in our absolute need to save ourselves from the moral decay and cultural Dark Age in which we have existed for so long. We can no longer afford to live with the virus of violence: it is literally killing us.

Today, despite having witnessed a black man sworn in as President of the United States, African Americans have become the most maligned and disrespected minority in the country. Every other week someone apologizes for making a racist remark and, yet, as a people, we are more preoccupied with the materialism of the day, and with hating each other, than with our collective social and cultural survival. We once commanded the position of vanguard for change in this country. The blood of our forbearers permeates the battlefields of every war this country has ever fought. But today, our collective spirit is broken and we must create ways to repair it.

We challenge you to take responsibility for yourselves and your neighborhoods. We challenge you to seize control over the forces in your lives. You don't lack intelligence, manpower, resources or creativity—what you lack is willingness. Each of us has the potential to make a positive impact. We need only choose to act.

To all emeritus Crips and Bloods, and other cliques, working for peace and change, we humbly thank you. Without your servant leadership and selfless commitment, any possibility for building a new paradigm would be unthinkable.

PART I:
BASIC AIMS & OBJECTIVES

Letter to my Homie

This is new for me to write to you like this, but it's the only way I can reach you for now. It's amazing to me how when I look at your generation, I can see a reflection of myself when I was younger. We all had our ideas on how to push a hard line so believe me when I tell you that I don't criticise how you function because I know you are trying to stay true to who you are and what you represent. I respect that. But I want you to think about something: being true to yourself and your hood also means change and growth. You're not the same person as you were at ten, none of us are. That's because, as human beings, we all possess the potential to grow and mature. So how you see things and think about things can evolve over time, and I'm certain you've already experienced this first-hand.

Your fierce commitment and loyalty to the hood is something I understand. When I was in the trenches, I felt the same way. So I would never ask you to abandon your hood and your homeboys.

However, what I will ask you to do is this: begin to have discussions with the homies about how to truly build your hood up. Since you're representing it, why not become a real investor in the growth and success of your neighborhood?

/continued

When I was young, I never thought about the hood as a place of political influence or economic prosperity, a place where I could actually own businesses and real-estate, but that's all changed, the world we lived in has changed, opportunities are everywhere and you can create success if you plan for it. Using the same commitment and determination you rep the hood with, you can make it a place you, your homies and your entire community can be proud of, a place where children can grow up without being afraid.

What I'm talking about is this: take stock of your hood, look around and ask yourself, "what can I do to make it better?" Take the initiative to change things, start having serious conversations with your homies and family about taking responsibility for the community you live in.

There is so much I want to tell you, which is why I wrote this letter. I wanted to give you a blueprint that will at least give you an idea on how to go about transforming yourself and your hood.

The first step for all of us if we truly love our neighborhood is to create some basic aims and objectives that will act a guide to reach your goals. I hope the following chapter will inspire you to map out a plan of action. If not you...then who?

Steve Champion

The Aim Of Gangs

"There's nothing wrong with being in a gang; it is the activities of the gang one should change..."
—Imam Warith Deem Muhammad

A major difference between street gangs and religious groups, political groups, military organizations, and unions is not so much an issue of collective behavior, but of the legitimacy of aims and objectives. So, the problem as we see it with gangs lies in the aims and objectives of the group: change the negative objectives and the negative stigma changes as well.

The aims and objectives of any group enable it to define itself as an organization, a fraternity, a society, a club, etc. We know that law enforcement, multinational corporations, prison guards, militaries, and even governments can all act, and have acted, gang-like, yet their stated aims and objectives give them legitimacy.

For instance: the aim of a government is to govern the affairs of the country; the aim of law enforcement is to enforce the laws of society; the aim of fraternal orders is philanthropy and good will; the aim of corporations is to maximize profits.

What are the aims of gangs? Of course, we can argue that the primary aim of a gang is to

15

provide a sense of belonging and recognition for kids and adults who are otherwise marginalized and powerless. If the primary aim for joining a gang is criminal activity, then real progress and advancement will never be achieved, and the cycle of chaos and failure will be the fate of every generation.

It doesn't make any sense to be a part of any group that doesn't have legitimate aims and objectives, goals, and a strategy for succeeding. Ask yourself these questions:

- Does your gang have a health plan?
- Does your gang provide legal services?
- Does your gang own real estate?
- Does your gang have a 401K?
- Does your gang offer life insurance?
- Does your gang give scholarships?
- Does your gang have a financial subsidy program for the homeboys and homegirls who get incarcerated, as well as for their families and children?

If you can't answer "yes" to even one of these questions, then you need to seriously re-evaluate what your gang stands for.

There's a reason the cycle of incarceration, death, drug addiction, fatherless and motherless children, school dropouts, and violence continues to affect generation after generation. It comes from a lack of vision.

Without a vision it's hard to develop a social theory, aims and objectives, build institutions, make progress, and welcome change.

Having shared objectives gives you the basis for reform and ideas about how you can achieve those objectives. Having a plan for reform makes it possible to correct past and present failures.

In order to change the current sense of decline and stagnation we need to set up organisations – in this book we call them Reform Boards – whose members are people like you. These Boards will develop policies and plans for community development in the areas of social, economic and political awareness.

A main reason gang members are indifferent to vandalizing and committing crime in their own neighborhood is because they don't feel anything in it belongs to them.

This means they also miss out on a connection to the larger community. So, the community itself *must* play a more proactive role in engaging gang members. Local Reform Boards can be a big part of making this happen.

The following graphic is a possible template for the responsibilities of a Reform Board

Reform Board functions

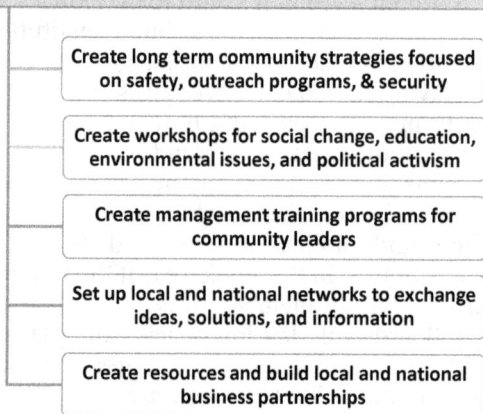

- Create long term community strategies focused on safety, outreach programs, & security

- Create workshops for social change, education, environmental issues, and political activism

- Create management training programs for community leaders

- Set up local and national networks to exchange ideas, solutions, and information

- Create resources and build local and national business partnerships

These are some of the practical steps a Reform Board will need to take to achieve development within the community

- Open a dialogue with gang members and invite them to join the reform board.
- Engage the people in the community to get involved in the community.

- Recruit people within the community who are skilled in business and community activism, so they can train people in these areas.

As things are now, each gang member tends to leave his or her life up to chance, wondering what to do and where he or she is going. But having real aims and objectives means that you can begin defining and transforming your reality and future. This is what *The Architect* is about — change that empowers you and the community.

Homie,

When something is broken, in order to fix it, you have to first identity the problem. Well, our neighborhoods are broken, homie. Everyone is tired of the same problems, day-in day-out; tired of the dead-end cycle of going to funerals, going to jail and going nowhere. Ok, so, here's the solution – change. Change how you settle conflicts. Change how the homies function and change how the hood operates.

You can do this by defining and creating a new agenda for your neighborhood. An agenda that encompasses owning businesses, being politically involved in the community, committing yourself to social and civil work. It's your hood, take care of it. Don't leave this up to other people because other people won't have your best interests at heart. You have to become the driving force of change in your hood. **/continued**

19

You can no longer stand by and do nothing when you know there's something that needs to be done. Don't make any more excuses and don't accept any. If you truly want to see a difference in your neighborhood, homie, get to work.

Craig Ross

The Need For A New Agenda

"Our nettlesome task is to discover how to organize our strengths into compelling power."— **Martin Luther King Jr**

We're not trying to address the whole of gang culture. That's too big and diverse to explore here. We're asking you to define and create a new agenda for yourself.

Where we specifically talk about the Crips and Bloods, that is due to our connection and familiarity with their culture and notoriety. It doesn't mean that we ignore the importance of other gangs and street soldiers who seek to redefine themselves and can benefit from this work. If we see culture as the behavior patterns, beliefs, traditions, and customs of a people or group, Crips and Bloods constitute a gang culture or subculture.

In order to redefine gang culture, we need a new philosophy and new attitudes. Gang members themselves must want to change and redefine who they are. They must be willing to overcome old attitudes and ways of thinking. As Ghandi said, "We must be the change we seek." The real origin of change is the individual.

Most of the peace efforts between gangs like the Bloods and the Crips have been largely unsuccessful. We believe the main reason for this is the lack of a real agenda. The first step in redefining what it means to be a Crip or a Blood— mere street gangs, or transformative organizations–has to be developing a real agenda and organizing individuals around it.

Like a deadly virus, the gangster's image has been transmitted from generation to generation. What if respected OGs and leaders within the Crips and Bloods got together and declared a new agenda like the one on the next page?

WE HAVE A NEW AGENDA—THERE WILL BE:

- *No more bloodletting*
- *No more committing crime in the hood or anywhere*
- *No more wasting our money; we are going to invest in the hood instead of destroying it*
- *No more using drugs*
- *No more being irresponsible husbands, fathers, sons, boyfriends*
- *No more hanging out in the streets doing nothing*

The new requirement for becoming a Blood or Crip isn't how many drive-by shootings you do, how many people you beat up, how many robberies you do, how many times you go to jail, or how many sexual conquests you have—the criteria is how intelligent you are, as demonstrated by going to school, acquiring a high school diploma or GED, and going to college for a degree, pursuing a vocational trade, or starting a business.

Today's gangs are not creating or building anything to ensure their survival. They are not building institutions, like schools, businesses, or think tanks. This shouldn't be surprising because they have no historical record to draw from as a model for building social, economic, or political organizations. Redefining gang culture, in the way nations rebuild after war, can profoundly change that.

Culture is the central glue that binds people together. It keeps them strong, focused, and united like European immigrants that left Europe throughout the 1800s and settled in America. They didn't come to America with financial wealth, but what they carried with them was their culture, and this made them ready to deal with challenges. It also enabled them to use the knowledge in their culture as a blueprint to build a new life for themselves and their children.

In contrast, when a people lose their culture or are unable to pass it **on, they inevitably suffer regression. This is seen in African Americans whose ancestors were enslaved from Africa. Their culture was systematically destroyed. They were prohibited from speaking in their native language and their history was erased from their memory.

Coming out of slavery, African Americans could only draw upon the limited knowledge and experiences accumulated in America and not the thousands of years of culture from Africa.

No culture is etched in stone, including gang culture. It is fluid and can change when new ideas are shared and take root.

When people praise the excellence in science and math displayed by Chinese, Japanese, and South Korean students, there is no wizardry at work. What we're seeing are highly motivated students whose cultures value education. Gang members, with a flip of a switch, could redefine their culture so that learning and excellence became the new standard.

It's time for gang members to undergo a profound change and redefine gang culture, to construct a new image based on advancement and excellence. It's time to expand your consciousness and develop an agenda—one that will empower rather than defeat you.

How To Create A Real Agenda

When a problem affects your life, you look for a solution. If the same problem affects the whole community, and even other communities, it's time to reach out to like-minded individuals and discuss what these problems are and what can be done to solve them.

Ideally, this can lead to solutions and plans of action around which people mobilize to address issues of concern. Here are some clear examples that show how creating a forum for dialogue and debate is an important first step for raising issues and solving problems:

- At the end of the Second World War, some perceptive leaders and individuals recognized a need for an international body to address global affairs. A series of discussions resulted in the creation of the United Nations. This international body constitutes a forum where heads of states can meet, discuss global concerns, air out their differences and grievances, and create solutions and strategies to global problems.

- In 1945, W.E.B. Dubois chaired the Fifth Pan African Conference in Manchester, England. One of its focuses was Pan Africanism (the worldwide movement to strengthen solidarity between all ethnic groups of African descent) and how to liberate the African continent. Attendees included Kwame Nkrumah and Jomo Kenyatta, who returned to Africa, freed their countries from European Colonialism, and became heads of state in their respective nations.

- In the 1960s, Huey P. Newton and Bobby Seale discussed what could be done to stop police brutality in their community. Their talks led to the creation of the Black Panther Party for self-defence and a ten-point program to address the social-economic-political needs of their community.

- Amiri Baraka, Charlie Diggs, and Richard G. Hatcher represented the steering committee that convened the 1972 National Black Political Convention in Gary, Indiana. One of the conference objectives was to discuss creating a black political party. Although no black political party was created, the following years produced political activism in the black community and a dramatic rise in the election of black officials nationwide.

These few examples show how discussions are essential to creating organizations. For the last forty years, the Crips and Bloods have been discussed in movies, books, music and symposiums by college professors, political pundits, law enforcement people, and community groups. Everyone has had their say...except the Crips and Bloods.

They're the ones who need to sit down and develop an agenda that stems from their own initiative, vision, consciousness, and intellectual growth. In the box below and overleaf are the five basic steps necessary for creating an agenda.

FIVE STEPS FOR CREATING AN AGENDA

1) *Groundwork*
   a. *Gather and compile information*
   b. *Talk to interested parties*
   c. *Fundraise to finance your plans*
   d. *Set up Regional and National Committees to organize workshops, seminars and conferences*
   e. *Choose representatives*
2) *Publicize*
   a. *Call for a regional and eventually a national conference or convention to discuss and analyze the critical issues confronting the black community*

---

    b. *This requires local and regional gatherings of gang members to discuss gang-on-gang conflict and violence and to devise solutions for making peace*
    c. *A national conference would also address such issues as economic development, political awareness and high unemployment*
3) *Define*
    a. *Outline shared aims and objectives*
    b. *Establish principles to abide by*
    c. *Create a shared agenda*
4) *Ratify*
    a. *Document the ideas agreed upon*
    b. *Create an organization*
5) *Return to your own community and lay the foundation for the work specified in the new agenda*

Let's be perfectly clear. When we talk about the need for defining, creating and building a new agenda, we are *not* talking about becoming sophisticated criminals. We are *not* talking about taking control over a street corner, a park, or a few city blocks. We *are* talking about changing the negative stigma towards gangs and becoming a positive and constructive force in the community, providing leadership, and being directly involved in the politics and economics within the community. This can't happen without defining and creating a new agenda.

Homie

I truly respect that you want the best for your neighborhood and yourself, so I'm obligated to tell you there is something you are going to need in order to do this; it's called a social theory.

In a nutshell a social theory is a blueprint that will connect all the dots for you. It will be the map you use to create change and success in your hood and in yourself. A social theory is basically no different than having a business model. It outlines everything you want to achieve and how to achieve it. It gives you an immediate advantage the moment you put it into motion because now you have a concrete plan that defines and organises your ideas and vision into clear strategies that will help you reach all of your goals.

What I'm telling you is this: you don't have to make it up as you go along. There's a better way to achieve the things you want to achieve. So, it's time for a new way of doing things. It's time you choose real transformation and real success over limited and temporary gains. When you've finished reading the chapter "The need for a social theory", you decide if you want your life to be controlled by mistakes you make or by the blueprint you use.

Steve Champion

A Social Theory

"When you have created a blueprint for liberation, then you have created a social theory."—**Steve Champion & Craig Ross**

A social theory is the basic blueprint for building self-reliant and self-sustaining institutions and societies. No nation can exist without one. The absence of a social theory leads to broken social institutions and civil chaos.

Creating a social theory involves addressing the social, economic, political, educational, and cultural problems that plague a nation, people or community.

Social theories are strategies aimed at taking control of and responsibility for a group's destiny in order to improve its welfare. It does three vital things:

- Replaces the "play it by ear" syndrome that many people live their lives by;
- Empowers you with a concrete vision; and
- Instills commitment and purpose.

A social theory is essential for any people struggling with systemic problems of growth, conflict, and cohesion because it builds and teaches values, principles, and objectives that are essential to progress and success.

- A social theory provides the solid foundation to develop aims and objectives in areas of social importance.
- Its primary function is self-development. There are no short cuts. Success is not accidental—it's planned. A social theory requires people to confront the challenges of their social environment and think of ways to bring about progressive change.
- A social theory also requires people to examine their own habits, behavior, and choices, and strive to develop their highest potentials. Functioning from a social theory leads not merely to a shift in one's actions, but to a shift in consciousness as well.
- Social theories can have different scopes, such as local, regional, national, and global. It might help to start with a local theory. It can expand as success is achieved at each level.

This understanding of social theory will guide you in making powerful and much-needed change and progress. It will increase your chances of creating safer communities and building wholesome relationships within them.

PART II:
THE TRIBAL MINDSET

"The tribal self is the level of consciousness that is shared by everyone who is a part of a particular 'tribal' experience."—**Dr. Naim Akbar**

Listen Homie

I'm going to speak on a sensitive subject. It's sensitive because I know cats start feeling some type of way when the words "setism" or "tribalism" come up. That's cool, I ain't mad at them. Hear me out, though. First, tribal mindset, hood mindset, set mindset, it's all the same. It's a group of people who are bonded by shared values, history, territory and loyalty. A group of people who look out for each other through thick and thin. This is the positive side, although you and I know this is not always the case. There's also a destructive and dysfunctional side to the tribal mindset. It's the toxic attitude of "us versus them" that grows from hood conflict and the hood stories that get handed down from one generation to the next. These stories, spoken like myth, become the dogma that shapes your thinking and influences your attitude about other hoods. Believe me, I know blood has been shed on all sides, but I also understand that no one has a monopoly on pain and loss.

/continued

Every day we see the hood wars send more bodies to the graveyard or prison yard. It's not hard to connect the dots, Homie, a quick reflection of your history will do that for you. If we are ever going to rise to our greatest potential, we must first move beyond the tribal mindset, which is our greatest weakness. You have to turn all assumptions on their head, homie, and sometimes this requires you go the extra mile in your thinking, but the end result is that you will no longer be dependent on a mindset that has only enslaved you.
Craig Ross

Moving Beyond The Tribal Mindset

History shows us the tribal impulse isn't some aberrant shift in human behavior. One of the humans' most powerful drives is the need to form groups. These social and familial groups began with clans, evolved into tribes, and eventually into religious sects, fraternities, and powerful kingdoms.

Gangs are sometimes described as "Urban Tribes." The problem street gangs and gang members have is that they remain stuck in a mindset that limits growth and change.

We don't disregard the anger many street soldiers carry as a result of loss and injury, nor can we forget the innocent lives lost as result of gang violence. It is for these reasons we support a

34

real process of reconciliation that offers the opportunity of peace, redemption, forgiveness, and respect. If such a process can be achieved in places like South Africa, Rwanda and Burundi, Liberia, Ireland, and Bosnia, then it can be achieved amongst Crips, Bloods, and other street gangs.

The greatest failure would be to do nothing and allow the tribal mindset to continue to be the deciding force in our neighborhoods and communities.

Based on our own experience as former gang members, over 30 years of research and countless conversations with gang members, we're confident that many street soldiers are tired of this dead-end cycle where life revolves around conflict, incarceration and death.

From all the letters we've received over the years from street soldiers, we know that many of them are broadening their worldview and taking on the challenges of change. They asked us questions like, "How can I change my life for the better?" "How can we set up a community program for our neighborhood?" or "How can we change the negative mindsets of our homeboys?"

Some of them have taken initiative by becoming involved in gang prevention and gang intervention organizations, or by joining community organizations with the purpose of improving their community.

We have met many street soldiers that are sincerely and tirelessly working to remove the tribal mindset of conflict and discord that has plagued their neighborhoods for far too long. Both Crips and Bloods, and other cliques, have come to understand that such conflicts are counterintuitive and counterproductive to lasting peace and progress.

This is the impetus many street soldiers have seized upon to transcend their present / past condition and resolutely commit themselves to true change.

Even so, gangs have yet to fully meet the challenge of change. Many remain trapped in protracted conflicts that are self-amplifying loops of attack and counterattack.

Since these conflicts are not about land, natural resources, liberation, religion, political power, or ideology, they have no real objectives. Violence simply becomes "something to do," "something to be part of." When a gang member gets up in the morning, his or her goal is to live for whatever is around the corner and whatever one can "get into."

To move beyond the tribal mindset, five negative states of consciousness must be recognized and replaced with positive states:

- Consciousness of failure: a belief that one cannot succeed.
- Consciousness of chaos: a mental state of confusion.
- Consciousness of apathy: a lack of emotional concern or interest.
- Consciousness of individualism: a state of self-centeredness and selfishness.
- Consciousness of self-hatred: a psychological hatred of oneself and one's kind.

Each of these negative states reinforces attitudes and behaviors that severely handicap personal growth - the psychological and emotional effects of living a life entrenched in conflict. Post-Traumatic Stress Disorder (PTSD) has been well documented in U.S. military soldiers, and many gang members show signs that are very similar to PTSD symptoms. When addressing the negative states and providing development and support, it is essential to address personal experience. Five positive states of consciousness can create attitudes and behavior that serve as the foundation for self-change:

- Consciousness of excellence: the belief to always expect the best of yourself.
- Consciousness of self-worth: recognizing you are of value to yourself, family, and community.
- Consciousness of integrity: always trying to do what's right based upon principles and ethics.
- Consciousness of industry: developing a strong work ethic to achieve goals.
- Consciousness of knowledge: valuing and pursuing education by all possible means.

Building a strong foundation for the future requires developing these ideals, principles, and mindset *now*, not later. Self-determination has always been the engine for forging and shaping a new paradigm. In the context of gangs, this means being able to detach yourself from static and self-destructive thinking and taking total control of your own socioeconomic, political, and cultural destiny.

With a high degree of resolve and fortitude, it is possible to become free from the tribal mindset. The choice for real change, or more of the same, is before you.

Homie

Let me give you some idea of what it means to empower yourself. It means taking full control of your life and making choices that will help you rather than harm you. It means not allowing other people to dictate the quality of your life or the outcome of your future.

It's unfortunate that there wasn't a model for self-empowerment created by the OGs. If there had been then your generation would truly have a legacy to build on. Well, we can't go back and change the past, but you damned sure can shape the present. You do this by taking ownership over the decisions you make, taking responsibility for what you do in your community and by holding yourself accountable for the actions you take. This is self-empowerment. It's not about net worth, it's about self-worth. Never confuse the two.

When you finish reading the self-empowerment chapter, become an example of what it means. Remember, you have a younger generation watching you. Give them something they can build on.

Steve Champion

Self-Empowerment

"Empowerment is something we must secure with our own hands."—**Steve Champion & Craig Ross**

Every Architect must yield to a greater call than him- or herself. Only then will he or she grasp the bigger picture. It is all too easy to fall into a cycle of day-to-day destruction. Only through self-empowerment do we find the courage to fight, build, and restore.

Self-empowerment starts in the home—when responsible parents instil in the child, at an early age, that he or she can be anyone or accomplish anything he or she sets his or her mind to. With this type of affirmation, the child grows up with a healthy sense of self-esteem and self-confidence.

The flipside—when there is a lack of support from family, friends and the community—can leave the child feeling disempowered and incompetent. This can create a lack of confidence that impedes the child's ability to successfully navigate the complexities of life, such as how to function in the workplace or how to negotiate interpersonal relationships.

History shows how individual acts can inspire and influence thousands of people. For

40

example, when Rosa Parks refused to relinquish her bus seat to a white male, she was arrested for it. Her defiant and courageous act did not only empower her, but was a catalyst that ignited the Civil Rights Movement, which in turn empowered tens of thousands of disenfranchised African Americans to take the streets and fight for their freedom.

Mass protest is the people's way of taking charge of their future. You have to decide how you are going to take charge of yours.

Even as gang members, we sought self-empowerment, but in the wrong way. Terrorizing citizens in our community, usurping control over a few blocks, calling the neighborhood park our turf, or loitering in front of vacant apartment buildings were not means to self-empowerment. None of these things helped us gain control of our destiny. Nor are they helping today's street soldiers and gang members gain control over theirs.

In order to become self-empowered and gain control over your destiny, you must figure out a way to direct decisions related to the economic, political and social systems that control your destiny.

As Malcolm X said, "This can only be done through organization."

Anytime you are socially, politically and economically disempowered, you cannot control your destiny. Gang members and street soldiers are disempowered in areas of social, economic and political power:

- Politicians create laws that stigmatize ex-convicts and felons by denying them employment, public housing, public benefits, voting rights and jury service—all of which amounts to social and political disempowerment.
- Politicians and lawmakers create rules that legalize employment discrimination and bar people from economic opportunities, and that's economic disempowerment.
- Gang injunctions target and prohibit gang members from entering certain areas in their neighborhood, which is social disempowerment.

The remedy is to create a self-empowerment program that encompass all aspects of life—including the social, political, economic, and spiritual.

Empowerment is the ability to make choices freely that serve your best interest. It is connected to human dignity and how one wishes to live his or her life. This is how we define empowerment:

- In education it means access to equal education—an education that teaches us to think critically and act decisively.
- In economics, it means having influence over the businesses and means of production in our community in order to create employment opportunities for those who live in the neighborhood.
- In politics, it means not just casting a vote and contributing money and energy to political campaigns, but supporting candidates who represent our self-interests, and negotiating for influence over political decisions that affect our community.
- In culture, it means creating our own value system, moral code and spiritual/religious practices in accordance with our cultural philosophy.
- In action, it means we must "back up" our ideas not with rhetoric but with commitment, determination, persistence and, more importantly, results and solutions.
- In relation to the self, it means, individually and collectively, we must teach people how to treat us. This can only stem from how we treat ourselves and others. If we carry

ourselves with dignity and believe we are great, people will treat us as such.

If we take the initiative and advance in some of the areas we have listed, our ability to profoundly transform our lives and become self-empowered in other areas would quickly follow. What we can't afford is inaction and a "let's see how it goes" attitude.

Inactive people who don't listen, think or speak for themselves tend to end up disenfranchised and disempowered. When someone is trying to take something from you, something you have worked, fought and sacrificed for, they are attempting to disempower you.

Public employees, like schoolteachers and fire fighters, can protest. For instance, they might protest about proposed legislation to abolish "collective bargaining."

Self-empowerment stems from self-knowledge. If we want to be free to determine our destiny, we must empower ourselves with knowledge of who we are and what our rights are. Empowerment must become our new mantra.

PART III:
POLITICS, ECONOMICS & EDUCATION

Hey Homie

I want to share some ideas I have about politics with you. I can't express it all in a single letter so the upcoming chapter will cover more ground. I also want you to give what I say some consideration. I ain't saying meditate on it, but just take it in and see if it lines up with what you have already been thinking about, then take it from there.

First, when I was growing up politics wasn't a topic of interest in my family. Actually, I don't ever remember it being discussed in my house, in school or at the church in my neighborhood. It was probably the same way in your house. Today, I can tell you I've grown some in my understanding of politics, but even so it can still leave a bad taste in my mouth when I look at what's going on in Washington. Yet I also know that, despite what I may think about politics and politicians, there's just no getting around it: politics affects all our lives whether we give a damn or not.

You've probably heard this before, but you can make a difference. How? By simply starting to learn about your neighborhood. What district is it? Who is the politician that represents it? Where do they meet? How can you contact them. How many votes does it take to win that district seat?

/continued

The answer to all those questions is one, maybe two, phone calls away – the equation is simple. If you really want to change things for the better in your neighborhood the first thing you have to do is exercise your right to speak up. If this sounds easy that's because it is. You gain political power through political participation. What gives people political influence is united effort. It determines who will be either on the inside looking out, or on the outside. You have to decide where you want to stand.

I don't expect you to change your thinking and jump onboard overnight. Change is a gradual process. My hope is that you read this chapter, like what you've read, and start to make small changes that will lead you to political action in your community. Maybe you are fed up with the social conditions in your neighborhood right now and want to do something about it, but don't know how and where to start. Well, maybe you know some of your homeboys who are already doing things in your neighborhood to bring about social change. Get with them. Don't just stand on the sidelines complaining about how things ain't never going to change. Hopefully, you can be inspired by "The Architect" and make a difference on your terms.

Steve Champion

Politics

*"Political power is the psychological relations between those who exercise it and those on whom it is exercised."— **Dr. Oba T'Shaka**

All human relationships are political in nature. We all need to make compromises, negotiate, be diplomatic, and manage our personal and social relationships much in the same way nations deal with one another.

Politics are inescapable in everyday life; even if you ignore them, politicians will continue to make political decisions and policies that directly or indirectly affect your life.

It's essential to understand and get involved in the local politics of your community and city so you can make real changes that benefit your entire neighborhood.

Without being organized and having a clear agenda, trying to impact political decisions at City Hall is like having a car without an engine. You won't get anywhere. But when you are organized into a political bloc, then can you exercise political influence. And a political bloc is simply a group of people or businesses united for a common purpose. For instance, what if the City Council decides to rezone areas in your neighborhood for toxic waste disposal or new

47

freeways, or pass an ordinance that limits the number of people in a group? What political influence will gang members have on these decisions? None at all, if they aren't politically organized. The logic is simple: if you are concerned about the politics that affect your life, then you can't complain about any changes City Hall dictates in your neighborhood. To have a voice, to make an impact politically, you have to be actively involved in the most important drama of your life — politics. See Appendix A for a more in-depth discussion of this point.

Homie

I want to start off by asking you, when you look around your hood, do you ever say to yourself; man, we don't own anything in our neighborhood?

If your answer is no, close the book right now, it can't help you. But seriously, if you said, yes, here's another question; how can you call it your hood when you don't own a single thing in it, not even a lemonade stand? Now, I know there's cats who got big money. They even own their house and a few businesses, but make no mistake, that's their stuff, not the neighborhood's. There's cats who will prosper while the hood itself is in bad shape, and while homies in prison struggle to survive. This is a lopsided equation because prosperity shared fairly across society should be the driving force for everyone who represents your hood. Anything less should be unacceptable.

The way you change this lopsided dynamic is to create a collective economic plan. <u>You</u> have to invest in your neighborhood. <u>You</u> have to get educated about business and finance. <u>You</u> have to make a commitment about developing a model that ensures every homeboy and homegirl who contributes to the hood will enjoy the prosperity of the hood. If you don't do this, you can't complain when other people start owning shit in your neighborhood.

Craig Ross

Economics

"History shows that it does not matter who is in power...Those who have not learned to do for themselves and have to depend solely on others never obtain any more rights or privileges in the end than they had in the beginning."
—Dr. Carter G. Woodson

One of the primary reasons gang members have failed to evolve beyond their problems is that they lack the knowledge to be economically successful in their environments.

Economic power is not a substitute for political power. You cannot control your destiny or claim self-determination if you don't control your economic life or possess the resources to negotiate from a position of strength.

You don't have to choose politics over economics or vice versa. You need them both. In hindsight, we can look back on the Civil Rights movement of the 1950s and 60s and see the emphasis was on political inclusion, but little attention was directed at building an economic base within impoverished communities.

The Civil Rights leaders in that era erred in thinking economic prosperity and mobility would follow after political inclusion. Although people did benefit from it, the vast majority of citizens did not climb the economic ladder. Thus, today, many communities throughout the country suffer high unemployment rates, economic deprivation, social alienation, and political exclusion.

Take a good look at the businesses in your neighborhood. Who owns them? Who owns the banks, supermarkets, the liquor stores, pharmacies, the clothing stores, the dry cleaners, the Laundromats, the fast food restaurants, the barbershops, the gas stations, the auto repair shops, etc.? Do the people who own these businesses live, shop, or spend their money in your hood?

How is it that you grow up in a community, claim a section of the community as your neighborhood, a neighborhood you are willing to die for, and yet you don't own any land or businesses there?

PEOPLE WHO TRIED "DO FOR SELF"

The philosophy of "do for self" in the Black community has been around a long time. Leaders such as Booker T. Washington, Marcus Garvey, Elijah Muhammad, Queen Mother Moore, and Minister Louis Farrakhan and others have advocated and practiced this philosophy. Former basketball legend Magic Johnson is following in similar footsteps with Magic Johnson Enterprises. His company invests in businesses across the country. He created the Urban Fund to revitalize urban neighborhoods.

Since 2015, members of the Dayton, Ohio community have cooperated to promote better food access in a hood where no stores sold fruit, vegetables and other fresh produce –the kind of food parents are told their children should eat but that can't be bought locally. The "Gem City" project began as a mobile food stall in one district. Now they're opening a worker- and member-owned full-service grocery store. To see local people working together to meet their hood's needs: https://gemcitymarket.com/about-us/about-gduci/

51

You cannot claim to be independent or free in your community without ownership or influence on the economy where you live. You can't claim, "This is my hood!" when your gang doesn't own anything there. You need to have legitimate economic investments in your neighborhood in order to fix its problems.

You are still just as economically powerless as the prior generation of your family members and your older homeboys. But if the philosophy called "do for self" was a part of the training and dialogue of your gang, your perspective about your hood and how you relate to it would be vastly different. But how can you "do for self" if you lack the necessary knowledge? The answer is obvious: acquire the knowledge!

It starts with you making a commitment to save your money and pull together your resources with like-minded individuals, the same way other ethnic groups do. These groups are not rich when they open a mom-and-pop store. But they save and put together enough money to get a small business going. You can't get upset when someone else decides to open stores in your hood. You must take the initiative yourself; if you fail to do so, someone else will.

We believe if you live in your hood and spend your money in your hood then you ought to work on owning businesses in your hood. When money is always taken out of your hood and spent elsewhere, a vicious cycle is created. "Less money in, more money out" results in the decline of the community. To show what can happen, check the box on the next page for a time when a black community flourished in the USA. Just imagine how prosperous your community would be today if the dollar circulated just half of what it did in Tulsa.

Living in a capitalist country like the USA requires capital. Developing an economic plan requires even more capital. In order for you to become self-reliant you must find creative ways to procure capital. One way to create capital is to set up a Business Cooperative right in your own neighborhood.

BLACK WALL STREET

In Tulsa, Oklahoma, from the early 1900s until June 1921, due to strict segregation blacks were allowed only to shop, spend, and live within a 35- square block called the Greenwood District. This community was so prosperous it was called Black Wall Street, or Little Africa. They estimate that each dollar circulated 36 to 100 times, sometimes taking over a year to leave the community.

On May 31, 1921, this successful black Greenwood District was completely destroyed by one of the worst race riots in US history. A 19-year-old black male accidentally stumbled on an elevator and bumped into the 17-year-old white female elevator operator, who screamed. Despite the girl's denial of any wrongdoing on the part of the man, it was falsely reported that she had been raped. That was all it took. White mobs gathered, then looted and burned all black businesses, homes, and churches. That was the end of Black Wall Street.

Why A Business Cooperative?

A business cooperative is a private business organization owned and controlled by the people who use its products, supplies or services. Cooperatives vary in type and membership size, but all were set up to meet their members aims and to adapt to members' changing needs.

You can start a business cooperative in your neighborhood, in a basement, church, mosque or garage. All you need is for you and another person to commit to saving your money. Here is how it works:

- Pool your financial resources (however much it is) with like-minded people by starting a fund that can be utilized for any business goals.
- The purpose is to build capital. If you save $100 every month and get four individuals to join you, at the end of the year, your business cooperative would have accumulated $6000. If you do this for three years, you would have saved $18,000.
- The more money you put into the business cooperative and the more individuals you bring into it, the more capital and purchasing power you will have.
- This might sound tedious, but the key to

successful financial security is having both short- and long-term goals.

- Once you have accumulated some financial capital, you have more options available to you. For instance, you can utilize your capital to open your own business; buy a house; lend money to other people who want to start a small business.

- Micro-lending involves small financial loans. Muhammad Yunus, author of the book *Banker to the Poor,* provides one of the best examples of this philosophy.

- Micro-lending can play a large role in offering financial assistance to struggling businesses in your hood. For example, if Chuck lives in the hood, owns a business in the hood, employs people who live in the hood, and needs a small loan to purchase some equipment for his business, he is a serious candidate for a microloan.

- The purpose of this kind of micro-lending is not to exploit businesses by putting interest on the money being lent. The purpose is to build up the community. Therefore, the principle loan is the only payment required. No interest should be attached. By understanding microloans, you can better understand how a business cooperative might work.

Make no mistake: it will demand a serious commitment, principles, and vision to build an economic base for self-reliance in your hood. Now is the time to take a long hard look at your life and your neighborhood and to take responsibility for both.

We wish someone had shown us how we could take charge of our lives by becoming economic leaders in our community. We could have transformed our neighborhood and, thereby, transformed our future.

You still have the opportunity to establish an economic foundation that can change the present course and help the younger generation. You still have an opportunity to take action and be a model of success. Every day you have the opportunity to transform your life and your neighborhood. All you have to do is make that choice.

Homie

My first six years of attending elementary school was an exciting time for me. I may not have been one of the smartest kids in the classroom but I did have a passion to learn.

/continued

By the time I got to Junior High this passion was practically gone. I'd begun to lose all interest in school. It was a combination of the teacher's inability to reach me and my growing belief that I didn't need school. With each new semester I cared less and less about paying attention in class, and while I still attended school, I had already mentally dropped out by the 9th grade.

Truth is, I stopped applying myself. Hanging out in the hood became more important. This would turn out to be a huge mistake. I didn't realise it at the time but giving up on my education actually meant I'd also thrown away whatever real possibilities I might have had for a better life. Noone had ever explained to me just how much of an impact getting an education could have on my life. I know now that education is the road that leads to whatever destination you want to go.

So, I want you to take a good look at our chapter on education because I believe it can help you get focused. The key thing is take responsibility for your future. I can tell you from personal experience that by making your education a priority, you open many doors of opportunity instead of shutting them.

Here's some food for thought. As human beings, we are by design learning machines. So don't accept the voice of your self-doubt, or the voices of haters, that you can't learn whatever grabs your curiosity and interest. Now, check out the chapter on education...go on.

Steve Champion

Education

You might think education isn't that important. Take it from us, it is. If you think having street smarts is enough to get you through life successfully, you are dead wrong. How many guys do I know who hustle in the streets who are financially successful? How many of them have stocks, bonds, or a retirement plan? Now count the number of guys you know who have gone to prison at one time or another and end up with nothing. Their numbers are countless.

Prison is filled with people (ourselves included) who once believed that reading books and getting an education wasn't important. We all thought hanging out with our homeboys, ditching school and hustling were our tickets to success. We used to crack jokes about kids who carried stacks of books to school each morning, calling them "squares," "hooks," and "bookworms." We failed to see that those same bookworms would be the ones who would become successful while most of the rest of us ended up in prison or dead. We not only closed the doors of opportunity for ourselves when we dropped out of school, we also cut ourselves off from the many life-enriching experiences higher education provides.

A college educated person makes 65 percent more over a lifetime than someone with only a high school diploma. Uneducated people don't have the same options and opportunities as educated people. If someone tells you that school isn't cool or important, and you don't need an education, that person is a liar and an idiot. If you want to increase your chance of having a better future in this world, you need to get educated.

What Is The Purpose Of Education?

The word education derives from the Latin *educere*, which means "to lead out, draw out, or bring out." So, the purpose of education is to discover the talents and creativity you possess and bring them to the forefront. This is what an education is supposed to do, not turn you into a mere robot. An education is not *all* about sitting in a classroom, digesting every word the teacher says, doing homework, and memorizing what you read in order to recite it. This might prove that you have a good memory, which is important, but it doesn't translate to education.

One of the things you are supposed to learn in school is to value curiosity and doubt. This means to think critically and learn to interrogate the world around you. From this, you learn how to skilfully manage your destiny, rather than having it controlled for you. Dr. Naim Akbar says, "A successful education equips you to gain control over the physical resources of the environment." In other words, a good education allows you to take full advantage of the economic opportunities and political involvement in the community where you live.

It's hard to argue that a state like California places a high premium on education when the state spends $62,300 a year to keep one inmate in prison, and just $9,100 per year per public school student, according to the California budget Project, a California think tank that studies fiscal policies. Based on these numbers, it doesn't take a genius to see what California's priority is. Even so, this shouldn't discourage you from pursuing an education. Education has to be a priority for everyone in our neighborhoods to ensure young people make the most of their time in school. We can never emphasize this enough.

The Importance Of College

Don't sell yourself short by believing the hype that college, higher education, is beyond your reach. It's not. We encourage you to pursue college and seek a college degree. The college experience, if you take advantage of it, will enrich your life. You will be surrounded by and meet people from all over the country and from around the world. You will meet and encounter people who have different perspectives that will challenge you to think beyond your viewpoints. You will be exposed to literature, politics, economics, science, art, and philosophy that will enrich you as a person and human being.

On the other hand, if college isn't for you, your education shouldn't stop. Education is a lifetime journey. You can seek it in other ways, like acquiring skills in nursing, computing, plumbing, welding, carpentry, etc. You might even want a vocation in community activism or volunteer work. Whatever you pursue, you should always be on a quest to learn more. If you feed your mind, it will grow, and you will grow. If you starve your mind, it will die, and your future will die.

Know Your History

We get it. Technology has shrunk the world, and we live in a global village. We understand that there is a human history that must be shared, but before you learn about other people's history, you need to know about your own history. Any time you know more about reality shows than about the history of slavery in United States, something is seriously wrong. If you want to understand something, you have to know its history.

It was once illegal to teach a slave to read and write in the United States; it was once illegal for women to vote, and marijuana was once illegal in all 50 states. The history of these and other issues now defines the society we live in. You need an education that not only looks forward but also looks back and challenges you to think and believe in yourself. You need an education that develops your humanity and your human identity, one designed to bring you under the influence of your own historical values, morals, and viewpoints.

We often place more value on things of no substance, and things that only give us temporary gratification, when we need to value the historical knowledge that can give us the skills and intelligence to solve our problems and change our future.

Knowing your history provides you with both a center and compass for the kind of direction, confidence, and focus you need to move forward and manage life in a productive manner.

Have you ever asked yourself why you and so many of your homeboys have a negative perspective about education? You have been spoon-fed lies and disillusioned about education for so long that you don't care much about it.

We were once the same way. You have to connect the dots and see education as a bridge that will get you to where you need to go and where you want to be. This is exactly what we did, even in our current situation.

When we were in school, more than one teacher wrote on the blackboard, "Education is the key to success." This is a profound statement that's supposed to convey the importance of education. Yet it was never explained to us *how* education could be the key to our success. You should know, whatever vision you have for your life, education improves your chance to succeed. We were told by our parents: "Go to school so you can get a good job." The message translated to our young minds that education equals money. It was only later we discovered that education and making lots of money are two separate things and don't always go hand-in-hand.

One of the keys to education is reading. When you read, it triggers imagination, it provokes thought, and you begin to question and research for answers. It broadens your scope and expands your horizons. As long as you are kept ignorant, you will never raise yourself to a higher level. Your mind can be easily manipulated if it is ignorant: not so a well-read mind. Ignorance is overcome by information and knowledge; and reading opens up the world to you.

The chronic illiteracy that plagues our neighborhoods and communities will be wiped out only when we make education a highly valued attribute of our cultural identity. It must become linked to self-esteem, to be seen as a truly desired personal achievement. When you acquire an education you naturally start to feel good about yourself. You become more self-confident and secure in your abilities to embrace and explore the world around you. You believe you can go anywhere and utilize the knowledge and skills you have to succeed. You realize that with your own will power you can accomplish anything.

In our own lives, we didn't have a positive school experience. By the time we were 12 years old, we had mentally dropped out of school, so that we were absent even when we were present in the building. It took us many years to realize that if you want a better life, education is the road to it. But you have to be willing to make sacrifices for it: that's the bottom line.

PART IV:
FRATERNITY

"Love your brother like your soul, guard him like the pupil of your eye."—**The Gnostics**
(Thomas 45)

Check it out, Homeboy,

At the risk of sounding dramatic, fraternity or brotherhood is the most powerful and most valuable principle we can practice because its core foundation is unity and having common goals. When real fraternity is shared it motivates everyone to cooperate with each other rather than compete against each other. The strength of fraternity harnesses the potential of each individual so they can effectively contribute to the whole. Imagine this level of teamwork and the success it can create. For years, hoods have been fighting against each other and, like in any war-torn country, it is always the people who suffer the most. They become trapped in a cycle of stagnation and underdevelopment. I don't have to elaborate on this. You see it every day in your hood – death, destruction of the family, drug addiction, poverty, imprisonment.

/continued

67

For decades, this has been the case in neighborhoods across the country, and in neighborhoods across the globe, for that matter. Where is the growth and prosperity for our neighborhoods? We can change this. We don't have to accept being at the bottom of the social caste system. With fraternity, we can make demands. When one stands with a million, a million stands up for one. I ain't saying it will be easy because it won't. You, me, everyone got to put the work in. Change is never straightforward or simple. In truth, we're trying to reinvent the wheel here, we're trying to do something that's never been done before. We're trying to create a new world...you feel me.

Craig Ross

Many gang members talk the rhetoric of fraternity, but their actions reveal profound contradictions. We witnessed this in the chaos of gang life.

For far too long the most negative qualities have flourished in friendships. The idea that Machiavellian traits are noble qualities is patently false. They are only applicable to men who want to nurture the worst in themselves and to coerce and manipulate others. For these men, fraternity is a mere situational tool to be used whenever it suits their purpose.

The true strength of all the fraternal orders has been the cohesion of a shared consciousness. It is this shared consciousness that nullifies the small ego and merges the individual with something greater than himself. One transcends his or her narrow perspective and expands to a universal one.

The philosophic and spiritual concept captured in the phrase "My brother's keeper" is linked to the ancient principles of fraternity. Today, we can see the fundamental principles of fraternity promulgated in the training and teachings of many of the world's leading institutions and organizations.

From ancient times to the present, the qualities of Brotherhood have survived, and some of them have survived in gangs that continue to practice principles like loyalty, commitment and unity. But within gangs these qualities have also become corrupted and estranged from their transcendental meaning. Today, relationships inside gangs are often opportunistic, parasitic, and materialistic.

We want to "shine the light," if you will, on true brotherhood, and point the way to a noble path, a path that many have followed for centuries.

When they're only based on convenience and superficial reasons, the bonds of brotherhood fail. Such relationships, cloaked in the guise of fraternity, are always defined by selfish motives, not a shared consciousness. This is why when tested or confronted with a crisis, these relationships usually end in the two people turning on each other. You don't see Freemasons killing each other or betraying one another like some gang members do.

WHY CALL THESE GROUPS FRATERNAL?

The idea of Fraternity or Brotherhood comes from our tribal past when the first hunting groups, warrior clans, and priest castes were formed to develop the skills and latent potential of each individual. This involved elaborate, often esoteric, initiatory rites that all beginners had to undergo. The rites were an ordeal to ensure that those who passed through each stage of the initiation would ultimately be transformed (or "born again") into a consciousness of brotherhood and sacred responsibility. Those who survived the test were referred to as "Brother." The knowledge that came from the early fraternal rites gave birth to more complex mystery teachings and secret societies that dominated the world's philosophic and spiritual teachings for thousands of years.

Imagine how different the behavior and mentality of Crips and Bloods would be if each of you had gone through this kind of change. Both gangs would be better able to deal with the challenges in your environment. All of you would have come to believe that you are your brother's keeper. Functioning from this reality, you would (and could) transform your gangs and your neighborhoods.

True fraternity affirms what is good and best in each other. Brotherhood doesn't excuse or turn a blind eye to bad behavior. When your brother is wrong, the philosophy and principles of fraternity teaches accountability. Clichés like "I'm down with the homie no matter what" only reinforce a lack of character and irresponsibility.

These two Bible verses illustrate key principles of fraternity, inspiration and sacrifice.

- *"Iron sharpens iron, so a man sharpens the countenance of a friend."*—**Proverbs 27:17**
- *"Greater love has no man than this, that a man lay down his life for a friend."*—**John 15:13**

In each of these there is a generosity of spirit that rises above ordinary friendship. True fraternity is extraordinary.

BECOMING FRATERNAL

The philosopher Pythagoras wrote, "Someone sharing your views and principles has more in common with you than a blood relative whose views conflict with your own." Only through developing our consciousness do we learn to see ourselves in others.

If your mind is firmly rooted in a fraternal consciousness, a change occurs—you are no longer a prisoner of "I" and "Me" egotism. Your thinking, attitude, and perception expand. You become a self-contained Architect of principles and values who reflects the best of fraternal integrity. Pythagoras understood that human nature clings to old habits.

Those who seek enlightenment and inner-change must be willing to give up their former self, to undergo a symbolic death. This death occurs when the individual passes through a personal crisis where he either breaks through his inner-schisms or continues in an unfulfilled (and "un-awakened") life. Those who break through their ignorance gain fraternal insight.

Malcolm X once said, "In order for someone to be your brother he must first act like your brother." The logic in this is clear. Only someone who has discipline over his own thinking and actions can act in your best interest. Only someone who understands the true meaning of brotherhood can behave as your brother. No one who has lied to you, manipulated you, and abused your friendship can value you or respect you as a brother because they don't value the principles of fraternity.

Calling a person "brother" or "homie" does not automatically make them one, any more than calling someone doctor or teacher makes them one. Without the necessary education and training, a person is simply making it up as they go along, playing it "by ear." This kind of false identity only leads to disappointment, time after time.

Fraternity, like any philosophy, must be learned. It is not grounded in status, power, fame, money, and materialism, but in the oldest of human virtues: sacrifice, trust, compassion, loyalty and honor.

But what if calling someone "brother" means you understand the meaning of "my brother's keeper," and you're prepared to practice and teach true brotherhood? Each individual must

73

locate with themselves the core and essence of their strength and principles. The principles of fraternity cannot be practiced halfway. To live the words "I am my brother's keeper," one's moral compass has to point towards a consciousness of brotherhood. This is the awareness we should live every day. There are no magic chants or shortcuts to true brotherhood.

Fraternity is all about the emergence and development of who you are as a person—psychologically, emotionally, and spiritually.

One of the great philosophical axioms is: "Within every life exists the seed of every life." Each of us possesses the seed to attain self-transformation and the consciousness of fraternity. It is up to you to undertake a personal journey that will elevate your consciousness, so you can take control of your own destiny. More on this vital subject in Appendix D.

Check it out, Homie

It has always been extremely difficult, if not impossible, for homegirls to take the leadership role in our neighborhood because the hoods have been largely patriarchal or male-dominated. This dynamic has to change, Homie. Respect and equality start at home first. It's vital that, when you start talking about creating a new agenda for your neighborhood, you include women at the decision-making table. They can no longer be mere silent supporters, secondary figures and obedient companions. They have voices, ideas and abilities that can and will greatly contribute to the transformation of your neighborhood and community. Working together as allies creates a synthesis of power and expands the range of people that you need to reach.

The women in your neighborhood have made immense and selfless sacrifices, you and the homies have to recognise and appreciate this. The role they've played over the years is immeasurable. Never forget the amazing women right in your own backyard. So, elevate your perspective about women, Homie, they are not your opponents, they are your sisters, mothers, homegirls, aunts and cousins. Have their back like they have yours, and you will have an ally for life.

I want to add, since my time in my prison and throughout my life, women have always been there for me. They deserve an honourable place in our struggle. This chapter on the role of women in the community will hopefully highlight that.

Steve Champion

Women In The Community

"If you don't like something, change it. If you can't change it, change your attitude."—Maya Angelou

Women are crucial to restoring hope and peace in

the community. They've always had to redefine themselves and create new mindsets for dealing with an ever-changing world. They have had to carve out roles for themselves in the workplace and community.

The role of a woman in the community cannot be transformed if she is locked out and denied a voice. Her role can only be a transformative one when she is given the same opportunities as men, and when she participates fully in the decision-making that defines and shapes the community.

Due to the dynamic in many inner-city neighborhoods plagued by rampant unemployment, high crime rates, gang violence and the mass incarceration of the male population, the women living in those neighborhoods are left behind to pick up the shattered pieces of their lives. They are left not only to manage their personal life in the rough terrain of their neighborhoods, but are required to maintain families, hold down a steady job, and become caregivers to both young and elderly relatives. Very often, they are charged with the responsibility of doing this alone. To deal with this challenge, it is so important for women to establish solidarity among themselves.

In general, women are the first teachers of children. They nurture our young, providing them with values, principles and wisdom. If women don't have the benefit of education and training, they cannot transmit it to the young. It is vital that men and women share the responsibility for ensuring that women have training and education that will advance them in all areas of life.

Malcolm X was a strong proponent of educating women. In one speech, he explained: "One thing I noticed in both the Middle East and Africa, in every country that was progressive, the women were progressive. In every country that was underdeveloped and backward, it was to the same degree that the women were undeveloped, or underdeveloped, and backward...in the African countries where they opt for mass education, whether it be male or female, you find that they have a more valid society, a more progressive society."

Women And Education

Education leads to opportunity. Opportunity leads to empowerment, which instills self-confidence, builds self-esteem, and gives men and women a voice and choices. These are important qualities to have in building a family structure, strengthening a community, and shaping a nation.

These qualities are especially helpful to women, due to centuries of patriarchal discrimination in defining what role they can play in the community. A community can be measured by how involved women are in its progress, development, and maintenance. The success or failure of any neighborhood or community around the world is deeply associated with what role women play in it.

Our assertion that women are the backbone of the family and community is confirmed by fact. Women have always been the glue that holds community and family together, particularly in times of hardship and struggle. The role of women in the community has been invaluable. We believe that the establishment of secure family households is one area in which women are most needed: secure family households lead to secure communities.

Women have proven they are leaders in their homes and families, that they are competent and capable of being leaders and pioneers. If communities are going to be rebuilt and transformed, women have to be inspired and empowered. Ideally, the inspiration and empowerment should come from them. But boys and men need to help them play a more active role in the community.

Empowering Women

Men can assist the empowerment of women by not discounting or obstructing their aspirations and, instead, by standing up for them. In many cases, this has happened when men have publicly spoken out for fair treatment and equal pay for women in the workplace.

When given a chance and a belief in themselves, women can achieve anything. When women decide to take control over their own lives and take initiative to fight for inclusion and equality, they become their own best and most effective advocate.

In some rural areas in Africa, Asia, and Latin America, where programs give microloans to women, the women have shown remarkable ingenuity and responsibility in investing in industries like textiles, shoe repair, pottery, agriculture, food stands, etc. The success rate of women repaying loans is high. But the real story here is that women are being empowered: they are raising their standard of living, building their self-confidence, and gaining the admiration and respect of family, friends and the community.

Here are some suggestions of ways our homeboys can help empower women and involve them in the community.

- One way of creating solidarity with women in the community is to start a study group, book club or social group.
- More men need to advocate and protest on behalf of women.
- Create a platform or focus group where men and women can dialogue on how to support each other.
- Support women's involvement in local politics. Encourage them to run for county supervisor, the board of education, or city council, and to join a political party.

However, we would also advocate that women look for ways to empower themselves, for example by taking up a cause.

Communities cannot achieve their full potential unless women are fully participating on an equal footing with men in terms of economic growth and political discourse in their neighborhoods. Issues like poverty, day-care, neighborhood safety, education, and affordable housing are important concerns for women. So is the creation of enterprises that give women viable means to raise themselves above the subsistence level. Without engaging women, these are not possible.

Involving Women In Community

In many communities, especially where gang activity is high, you can find women who have lived in the same neighborhood all their lives. Some of the women raised their children in the home they grew up in. Even though these women have lived in the same neighborhood for 30 or 40 years and witnessed the decline of their neighborhood, they have never taken an active role to change the social conditions there.

This isn't because these women don't care about their neighborhood. They care a lot. Many of them have been touched, in one form or another, by tragedy. A loved one, a close friend or an acquaintance has been shot, murdered or incarcerated. Some of the women have been victims of violence themselves.

There are many reasons why women aren't active in their communities including the stress of family life and that working a full-time job leaves little or no time, especially for a single mom, to do anything else. It's estimated there are over ten million single moms in the U.S.

Women also are not being actively encouraged to get involved in the community. We know women join organizations like a gang prevention or intervention group but end up being marginalized. These organizations are male-driven, and the women usually take a backseat to dominating men. Issues concerning women are not the focal point of the group. There's a lack of leadership roles for women within these organizations so their concerns aren't being expressed.

We've talked with women about political involvement in their communities. Many of them would like to get involved. However, they are not being socially engaged nor do they have a clear vision of what they can do, so a lot of women remain silent.

Men must be more proactive in engaging women. We must reach out to them. We must solicit and encourage their ideas, input and feedback. We must have a robust dialogue on what needs to be done in the community. We must have a conversation about issues concerning women and what role we can play to support them.

We might even need to go door-to-door to talk with and engage women, in the same way southern Civil Rights activists in the 1960s went door-to-door to register African American voters to vote.

Social reconciliation and social repair in the community cannot occur without women. Lasting peace and community prosperity cannot be achieved until women are empowered, engaged, and become agents for creating sustainable communities.

The role of women cannot be determined by anyone except them. Women make up the other half of the struggle—they are our grandmothers, mothers, sisters, aunts, daughters, cousins and nieces. They are our friends, our neighbors and our co-workers. They cannot be neglected or dismissed. They deserve the support of men.

When women in the community forge a strong group, they become a formidable force, enabling them to transform their communities. But the first change must start with women themselves. They must have a shift in consciousness and develop a new awareness of their role in the community.

Homie

For a long time now it seems to me, maybe to you too, that somewhere, at some point, the meaning of real brother and sisterhood got lost. Correct me if I'm wrong, has it stopped being about personal accountability and now is about "I do my own thing"
/continued

with no regard to accepting responsibility. Is selfless giving a thing of the past because having a false sense of self-entitlement is the new trend?

Does having real ethics identify you as outdated because doing whatever the situation calls for, then calling it gain, is the new upgrade? This cannot be the definition of keeping it real. This is why this chapter is so important because it defines and reaffirms the highest standards of true brother and sisterhood.

Ethics are to brother and sisterhood what the steering wheel is to the car. Without ethics you will not be prepared to choose the course of your life. You'll just be reacting to whatever fate comes your way. Having a code of ethics outlines how you should conduct yourself and deal with problems be they family, friends or strangers. When brother and sisterhood is practiced with ethical values it supports the welfare and solidarity of all, not just the individual.

Every day you see hypocrisy from cats who call you homie but don't live the principles you embrace and uphold. The very concept of brother and sisterhood is rooted in common experiences and shared ethical values. When these ethics become diluted, how can you honestly say, "I am my brother's keeper."

The highest ethical principle is integrity, Homie. This is the jewel in the crown of brother and sisterhood. It leads you to a higher understanding and a higher purpose.

Craig Ross

Maat, Brotherhood and Sisterhood

"It is not good but righteousness by which people are sustained."— **Ptah Hotep, Vizier of King Isesi**

Maat is an ancient Khemetian (Egyptian) ethical system that was created between 4000 and 3500 BCE. It is the oldest ethical system known to humanity. The ancient Khemetians built a civilization that was once the shining light of the known world—it was based on Maat. These same ethical principles are indispensable for social and moral development in brotherhood and sisterhood.

Maat has multiple meanings, but the standard meaning is truth, justice, and righteousness. It can also mean harmony, order, and reciprocity.

Our objective here isn't to write a dissertation on Maat. Our objective is to answer the following question: How can Maat be applied and utilized to build a strong brotherhood and sisterhood?

Brotherhood and sisterhood mean a community, not just a band of individuals. Each individual is a person in that community, in the same sense that each individual is a person in a family. What makes these relationships special is how each individual treats and interacts with the others.

Maatian values of truth, justice, and righteousness will build a strong and lasting brotherhood and sisterhood. Those who love and practice these values will find brotherhood and sisterhood around them. By applying the virtues of Maat in brotherhood or in sisterhood, your life will be transformed.

The equality in brotherhood and sisterhood lies in the ethics of Maat. A relationship rooted in Maat is a relationship where people relate as one soul and one consciousness, regardless of wealth, race, and class. When each person in a community of brotherhood and sisterhood thinks about, upholds and lives these values, they become the temporal embodiment of Maat just as those who go through communion become the temporal embodiment of Christ. Therefore, Maat becomes a pattern for how brothers and sisters live their lives. If you'd like to learn more about Maatian ethics, read Appendix B.

Part V:
Spirituality

"The true essence of all spiritual teachings is practice and balance."—**Ross, Champion, & Williams**

Homie

I'm not about to preach to you, or anyone else, about which God or religion is better. I was raised in the Black church so I know first-hand how the subject of religion can start heated arguments. I believe whatever religion you choose to practice, that's your business. I also believe that two intelligent people can always find common ground. When we talk about the need for spirituality we're talking about some pretty basic principles: unity, balance, humanity, and oneness. Sometimes religious faiths don't do a good job getting this message across. It gets lost in the dogma. But the common thread of spirituality is being connected to your own humanity, that divine energy that exists within all of us, so that you can feel empathy, compassion and understanding.

There's a saying, "If you do not believe in something, then you stand for nothing." Everyone needs an anchor, be it faith or science. This is what gives us the inner strength to endure.

/continued

I can tell you from personal experience that my life has focus and balance because of my spiritual path. It has given me a sense of purpose that I never had years ago. I want this chapter "the need for spirituality" to shed some light on a topic a lot of homeboys try to avoid, but more importantly I want all homeboys to know having a spiritual path or a religious faith is OK.
Steve Champion

The Need For Spirituality

When we talk about spirituality, we are talking about the domain where we recognize our oneness and unity. Most religions are conceived for the purpose of bringing people together, showing people how they are one. Religion tries to teach us that our differences should not transcend our humanity.

Spirituality is about coming into the knowledge of self. It's about living in accord with our essential nature and understanding the fundamental purpose of our being. It's about looking inside ourselves, not outside, for the spiritual power that we generate when we come into a consciousness of spiritual truth.

History shows that spirituality has been and continues to be an important anchor sustaining African people for millennia. It has enabled them to survive and overcome the most unspeakable horrors in the most difficult times.

From an early period of human history, African people have never needed anyone to instruct them on when to be spiritual. We live it in our daily lives. We didn't have to discover spirituality in a book. It was already written in our hearts and rooted in our consciousness.

We knew we had spirituality within ourselves—thousands of years before Moses presented the Ten Commandments; before the Buddha sought enlightenment; before Socrates told his students "Know Thyself"; before Jesus said, "The Kingdom of Heaven is within." Our ancestors of ancient Khemet (Egypt) wrote on their temples 4,000 years ago in hieroglyphics: "Man know thyself." This was one of the first philosophical concepts to guide African people's consciousness.

We understand that everyone walks through different doors searching for inner peace and spiritual harmony. We don't think it's important *how* you get there – just that you get there. Some people find what they are looking for in traditional African spirituality, or in Hinduism, Buddhism, Judaism, Christianity, or Islam. Some find it in other sacred spiritual traditions. You might find it in all of the religions. You might also come to realize that what you need is right where you have been standing all the time. Whatever speaks to your spirit and enables you to realize your potential—that's what you should practice.

Some people have suggested that due to their antisocial behavior gang members are spiritually dead. We do not believe that. We do believe, however, that they are spiritually misdirected. They have the potential, just as everyone does, to live spiritually fulfilling lives. The problem lies with the misdirection of their spiritual energy. Energy doesn't distinguish between good and bad, between positive and negative. Energy follows thought and is like fuel to an engine. If the mind gives rise to corrupt and destructive thoughts, our actions will be reflective of that energy. We must gain control of our spiritual faculties so that we are anchored in a moral direction.

We come from a religious background, but as we grew older, we moved away from religion. We could readily admit our belief in God and name our faith even though we were immersed in criminal and gang activity. We also knew gang members who would openly declare their religion but say they were not actively practicing it. They believed that once they accepted a religion, they would find spirituality, but we discovered it works in reverse. Discover your spirituality first, and then search for a religion to match it if you can. The Buddha says: "If this path does not work for you, try something different."

There is no need for gang members to reinvent the wheel by creating a new spiritual system. But whatever religion or spiritual system you adopt, you have a responsibility to transform it, so that it speaks to the needs and conditions in your life—relates to where you are and want to go. This is one of the most fundamental and important aspects of any spiritual system: that it can and does speak to the needs of people during the present time.

Another important aspect of spirituality often overlooked is the lack of attention we pay to our modern-day shamans. A shaman is someone who has had a psychological and transcendent experience and has been transformed by it. They are people who interpret the world around us in a way that gives a deeper understanding of ourselves, of humanity, so that we can fully engage with life. For instance, the late, esteemed poet Maya Angelou and the well-known writer of mythology, Joseph Campbell, spent their lives teaching and inspiring others to become better human beings—or, in Joseph Campbell's words, "To find your bliss."

One of the things that every spiritual teacher, past and present, leaves us is a glimpse into the spiritual life via their writings and the example of their personal lives. In the Gnostic gospel of Thomas, Jesus says: "If you bring forth what is within you, what you bring forth will save you." But during most of our juvenile and early adult years, what we found inside ourselves and brought forth, like many people of our generation and beyond, was a consciousness of self-destruction. We had no knowledge or understanding that we possessed inside ourselves breadth and depth that could transform our lives. Only once we came to understand this were we able to become our potential, and essential, selves.

Homie

We all know, and can agree upon, our neighborhood's got major problems. The question is, where does the solution come from? Well, don't expect politicians to come up with anything that's going to be in your favor. Whatever options are put on the table have to come from you. You have to come up with the answers or nothing is going to change. You have to start to unpacking this shit because you got a front row seat in the trenches and see first-hand what's going on. What I can tell you is this, problem-solving requires you to look at a problem from different angles, different perspectives. You do this by making sure your ego don't get in the way of what is best for your neighborhood first. There has to be a shift in your consciousness and it begins when you make your neighborhood and community a priority.

This chapter is about shifting your thinking and your attitude so you can devise the transformation you want to see in your neighborhood. All kinds of people want to use your youth, your energy, and if they can't exploit you then you are useless to them. It's time you take control of what happens to you. Only then, Homie, will you see real change in your hood.

Craig Ross

A Shift In Consciousness

"Obstacles and resistance exist in consciousness and therefore can be cleared away."—Deepak Chopra

To exist in a static consciousness means the following: no personal growth; no vision; no long-term planning (just short-term goals and limited gains); no objectivity; and a lack of emotional maturity. Such a consciousness results in an absence of creative energy and repeated mistakes.

Static consciousness is a primary reason why there are a lot of adult men who act like they are kids. We're not talking about guys who are comedians; we're referring to grown men who have failed to make the emotional and psychological transition into adulthood. We have all seen and know these men—men who live in a consciousness of chaos, failure, selfishness, defeatism, and rejection of any responsibility and accountability.

Now, no amount of complaining and theorizing has ever fixed anything. Problems do not solve themselves and solutions do not miraculously appear out of thin air. It all begins with the individual having a consciousness that thinks beyond the confines of the norm and engages the creative process. But in order to do this, a shift in thinking must occur.

What Is A Shift In Consciousness?

It is a real process that can take place anywhere, at any time to anyone. To "shift" means to *move*, *alter*, or *change* the direction, position, or place of something. "Consciousness" is the awareness and understanding of self, environment, and purpose.

One recurring lament we have heard over the years goes like this: "Things are fucked up. There's no collectivity. No advancements. No real progress. A crisis of leadership. Things ain't never going to change."

While the bulk of these claims can hardly be argued with, if everyone believed things will

94

never change, then no one would ever try to find answers to the problems or commit themselves to making a difference. Yet people do these things on a daily basis, despite the challenges, the odds, the negativity from naysayers, and the lack of resources. They do it because there's been a shift in their consciousness and they believe in something more, something better.

Albert Einstein said, "You cannot solve a problem with the same consciousness that created it." This maxim describes the very need for a shift in consciousness. In order for problems to be solved, the thinking responsible for it must change, and for thinking to change, consciousness *must* change first. It is that fundamental.

Try this: turn off the lights in your room for about 15-20 minutes. Stare into the darkness. Your pupils dilate and you see nothing, right? Try to move around without being disorientated. You can't, right? When you turn the lights back on your pupils will narrow as they make the adjustment to seeing again. Your movement is confident because you see everything clearly. A shift in consciousness is similar. It's about making adjustment in your thinking and your perception, so that you change from less effective actions to actions that produce desired and effective results.

Perception creates reality, and if you want your reality to change, then change your perception by a radical shift in your consciousness.

Achieving a Shift in Consciousness

Like everything in life, a shift in consciousness is a process. One that begins the moment you decide self-change is needed. There is no specialized training you need to undergo. No deep meditation or chanting to do, no ancient text you need to read. All it takes is your *willingness*, your *determination,* and your *attitude*.

Your willingness is your sincere drive and commitment to pursue goals and take initiative. Your determination is having a clear purpose, creating expectations for yourself, and helping to empower those around you. Your attitude is how you respond to people, challenges, situations, and the life you live.

The most important of the three in achieving a shift in consciousness is *attitude*. If you resist self-change because of your attitude, then you won't ever accomplish any objectives you may have because success demands an elevation in thinking. It's that simple. Had Malcolm X had the attitude that he didn't want to hear anything Elijah Muhammad had to say, he probably would never have been willing to undergo a shift in consciousness. The fact that he did experience a shift profoundly impacted the social history of America. His story truly exemplifies how none of us can know the depth of our potential until we achieve a shift in consciousness.

Here are three basic steps to creating a shift in your consciousness:

- Be willing to listen.
- Be willing to change your attitude.
- Be willing to ask questions.

Some of your biggest mistakes will be the ones you make carelessly, without thinking. We have been guilty of this. We have also learned this can be prevented by understanding how your thoughts inform your intentions. Being aware of your thinking will produce insight, which will lead to a shift in your consciousness.

Benefits Of A Shift In Consciousness

When consciousness shifts, so too does provincial thinking. It changes how you view and evaluate things. It sharpens your logical reasoning. This is the case for many people.

The life of Buddha is an example. He was born into royalty and lived a charmed and stress-free life. Once he ventured out in the world and saw the suffering around him, his consciousness changed, and he was inspired to go on a journey. On his journey he became enlightened and created philosophical teachings based on his experiences. Today, over a billion people follow his teachings.

Stanley Tookie Williams, a founder of the West Side Crips, spent over 20 years on San Quentin's death row. During this period, he began reading and studying. His consciousness grew, his insights deepened, and he transformed himself. Then, through his celebrated anti-gang books, he warned kids not to join gangs. Without a shift in consciousness this could not have happened. Nor would it be possible for us to write about or have a conversation about consciousness without our own self-transformation. A shift in consciousness infuses you with a sense of something higher than yourself.

We are all, to varying degrees, conditioned by our environment. If our home environment and/or our community are deficient in the striving for excellence and the achieving of success, and if due to lack of opportunity and broken promises, distrust and disillusionment are rampant—all this negativity will be reflected in us. Our dialogue with young gang members has made it clear that they don't aim for the stars or believe they can succeed at anything legitimate because they haven't been told on a consistent basis that they can. A shift in consciousness can change this.

A shift in consciousness can overcome environmental conditioning. People do it every day. They have a moment of clarity, or an epiphany, or they are tired and fed up with the same old story that goes nowhere, and they choose change over being static. How many times have you looked back on your life and wished you could do things differently? How many times have you said to yourself, "There has to be more to your life"? How many times have you thought about the problems around you and felt things needed to change?

This is why a shift in consciousness is so important: it gives you the wisdom to come up with answers, to spot problems before they become problems, to resolve contradictions and make intelligent choices.

People who are satisfied with their false sense of comfort live in an ignorant bliss. But too much bliss leads to a coma. In a coma, one doesn't have the ability to think, make decisions, or even move. This is what happens when our thinking becomes static. We lose our ability to think, to make effective decisions, and to act with purpose. Being static severely limits any progressive motion; a shift in consciousness restores it.

The primary benefit of a shift in consciousness is that you are transformed into someone who builds, someone who can create change, and this is the essence of being an Architect.

A shift in consciousness develops character, creates a sustained feeling of mission, self-worth, and awareness. You learn to control your emotions, your ego, and your reactions. You eliminate dead aspirations and the consciousness of failure.

You are no longer confined to one-dimensional thinking but are able to use critical thinking, which widens your perspective and gives you self-control over negative impulses.

A Rite of Passage For Building Manhood

"When I was a child, I talked like a child, I thought like a child, I reasoned like a child. When I became a man, I put childish ways behind me."—1 Corinthians 13:11

Homie

What if, when you were 12-13, you went through some kind of training or orientation that prepared you for the realities you had to deal with every day in the neighborhood? Well, one thing for certain, you would have been much more equipped to handle the daily obstacles and pitfalls that came your way.

I'll be the first to tell you that every hardship you've endured could have been predicted, and more importantly, it could have been prevented. This is why a rite of passage tradition in our neighborhoods is so important. It teaches the youth vital lessons they can effectively use in the community. It gives them the necessary tools to make choices that benefit them. I'm not saying a rite of passage is the cure for all the problems in our communities. Some of that stuff falls on our shoulders. But if we had a rite of passage tradition in our neighborhood, we would be in a much better position to guide the youth on a more constructive path. That's just a fact. It's a crying shame when the youth of your neighborhood have to look to rappers and celebrities and ball players as role models, and not the faces they see every day right in the hood. This dynamic has to be changed, Homie. We owe the next generation more. We owe today's generation now.

Craig Ross

The Meaning Of Manhood

It is taken for granted that a person born male will automatically grow up to be a man. Not true. Maleness is a matter of gender and is in no way indicative of manhood. If it were, there wouldn't be so many thirty-, forty- and fifty-year-old males posturing as men but behaving like irresponsible little boys. Since there is no seminal point in a male's life that declares him a man (other than physical changes like the growth of facial and body hair, the change in voice and the increase in height) males are, for the most part, unsure as to when they become men. We suggest that a male must *intend* to become a man, and that this is facilitated through a rite of passage that involves engendering a strong sense of identity and teaching the young male the ethics of responsibility and purpose.

The vital lessons learned in a rite of passage prepare the individual to become a contributor to his family and community and for existing within human society. The rite of passage both defines and teaches manhood.

In the U.S. there is no national tradition of a rite of passage. Although some ethnic groups do practice one within their own culture, African Americans as a whole do not observe one. Some scholars have argued that if African Americans had a rite of passage tradition, many of the problems plaguing black communities would not exist. Whether or not this reasoning is valid, the truth is, something is better than nothing.

Many of the social problems communities face such as youth violence, teen pregnancy, high dropout rates, drug abuse and gangs may, arguably, be attributed to the absence of a rite of passage. We are not suggesting that young males should be taken into the wilderness to hunt and kill animals or engage in a bloody gladiator battle to prove their masculinity. We're talking about a rite that would have a profound and transformative effect on the spirit, character, and attitude of the young person.

In order for a boy to transition into manhood he must first go through the process of maturity and self-realization. Doing this he learns to develop aspirations, a moral compass, and an awareness of who he is. Once he becomes aware, his perception shifts, and he lets go of his boyhood. He is no longer the boy who began the journey, but the man who completed it.

We have outlined three common themes that occur throughout history that define the inward journey for self-discovery: the departure, the initiation, and the return.

1) **The Departure** symbolizes the beginning of the inward journey we must take in order to achieve self-discovery. By journeying inwards, we purify the self and connect with the source of our own being
2) **The Initiation** symbolizes the training, studying and enlightenment we experience on the journey, and includes the death of our old self and the birth of our new self.
3) **The Return** symbolizes completion. The spiritual return for us having undertaken the inward journey provides a new value system and requires us to be an example of our transformation.

A person going through this process is called an initiate. On their journey, the young male initiates would learn about conflict resolution, fundamental values, and principles such as integrity, respect, commitment, accountability, and responsibility. They would be encouraged to get involved in the life of their community, and taught about environmental issues, politics, community organization, entrepreneurship, and volunteering. Following completion of a rite of passage, the young male would have taken a crucial step into adulthood.

In a male's life there are different transitional periods that occur. For this very reason, we believe that there should be three stages to the rite of passage. The first encompasses the years from age 11-13; the second spans ages 14-17; and the third is for age 18 onwards (the adult level.)

First Stage Rite Of Passage, Age 11-13

By "rite of passage," we are referring to a ritual process symbolizing the transition from adolescence to spiritual, intellectual and moral responsibility and maturity. A rite of passage should include:

1) A physical/mental ordeal or test. The individual might test his endurance by performing a series of exercises like completing a decathlon or running a marathon. He might sit silently, fasting throughout the day. He might go on a solo spiritual retreat and visit a spiritual center, a sacred spiritual/religious site, a national park, or just camp outside to enjoy nature and contemplate his own being. He might also perform some missionary work.

2) A symbolic death. The initiate is taught that in order to be renewed and reborn, parts of him must die—immaturity, ignorance, bad habits, and his old self.

3) A symbolic rebirth. The initiate is reborn into a consciousness of cultural and spiritual awareness, leadership ability, commitment, purpose and responsibility. He is renewed.

The initiate must also learn about conflict resolution and be instructed in fundamental values and principles such as discipline, loyalty, integrity, respect and commitment. He must show fundamental knowledge in:
1) Social environment: awareness of community leaders, organizations, governmental programs, local events, educational opportunities and social services (for example, law enforcement, fire department, 911 emergency.)
2) Economics: awareness of community business leaders and owners, employment opportunities and how to manage money.
3) Politics: awareness of the three branches of government (judicial, legislative and executive) and how they function; awareness of local political parties, politicians and leaders; awareness of how governmental affairs directly affect the community.

Having successfully passed through the first stage of emotional and mental maturity, the initiate has taken a crucial step in making the transition from boyhood to young adulthood. Mentoring reinforces what has been learned.

Second Stage Rite Of Passage: Age 14–17

The purpose of this stage is to provide vital guidance and mentorship to this critical age group helping them to navigate the daily challenges and obstacles they will confront.

It is important to create a program that addresses the unique needs of this age group. Here we give several examples:

1) Learning impulse control – thinking before acting.
2) Taking responsibility for oneself – understanding the consequences and weighing all options.
3) Practicing discipline - self-control and self-motivation.

It is absolutely necessary to expose this age group to a wide range of positive experiences that broadens their world view, elevates their self-confidence and shows them the possibilities and opportunities that are out there. It is equally important to give this age group simple principles and ethics they can understand and live by. This will be the foundation of their decision making as they go into adulthood.

Key takeaways :

1) Emphasize higher education, but also cultivate creativity and talent.
2) Teach a philosophy of succeeding against adversity.
3) Focus on mental and emotional wellbeing.

We believe this age group is essential to the positive growth, peace and health of the neighborhood and community. Creating a rite of passage that sustains them into adulthood is the fundamental duty of all neighborhood leaders and OGs. To neglect them would be akin to treason.

Third Stage Rite Of Passage, Age 18 +

We believe this stage is needed for adults who have not undergone a rite of passage previously. It not only acts as an example for the younger generation, but it also serves as a social bond, and recommitment to the responsibilities we, as adults, have to our families, friends, community and neighborhood.

The adult rite is ceremonial. The ceremony and activities must be created by each neighborhood. There should be three main goals:

1) Acknowledgement of duty to the community.
2) Renewal of commitments.
3) A firm resolve to build positive change.

Adults who sign up for the induction into the second level rite of passage must be able to demonstrate contributions to the neighborhood, community and leadership initiative in one or more areas:

1) Social or political activism.
2) Entrepreneurship.
3) Business.
4) Philanthropy.
5) Community leadership.
6) Personal transformation.

The primary aim of the adult rite of passage is to have leaders and OGs who are all on the same page with the same objectives. You not only need leaders who can uplift and inspire those around them, but leaders who can show compassion, love and integrity to their community and neighborhood.

In conclusion, undergoing a rite of passage is like walking through a sequence of doors; at each door the initiate learns something about himself and the world. He sees things he has never seen before. He is forced to re-examine his life. He comes to the realization of who he is, and he recognizes his new role and responsibility. His attitude, thinking, and behavior are no longer those of a child, but of one who has matured. He has shed his immaturity and emerged as a socially mature being. He becomes an Architect of Change.

PART VI:
INSTITUTIONS & COLLECTIVITY

OK, Homie

I'm going to jump right to it: what is an institution? It's an organisation, a foundation, a society, churches, or anything with similar function that provides sustainable development and constitutes the basic standards for rule of law and social values for business and people. Now, next question: why are institutions important? Because they can transform nations, societies, communities, and neighborhoods, homie.

When you first hear the word institution you automatically think it has something to do with the government or some global organization, right? Well, there is a local approach to institution building and I want this chapter to encourage you to start putting your ideas into practice. I want you to be inspired enough to develop your own vision. Don't ever underestimate yourself, Homie, you just have to think in alternative ways. Building an inclusive, effective and accountable institution requires an unbreakable resolve, commitment, patience, and a great deal of elbow grease. People will want to see you fail—mostly I'm talking about cats who are addicted to chaos and misery. You know who they are. Don't let them undermine your efforts. You got to stay focussed, Homie. I've been telling you this for a while now.

/continued

Anyway, there is no one size fits all approach to institution building. That would be downright lazy. Do some investigation. Start taking stock of the specific problems in your neighborhoods and the things you want to see happen. Grass roots solutions are community-based solutions and you are a reflection of your community, so why not you?

Oh, one last note before you dig in; never overlook the fact that people make up institutions and they come with their own human weaknesses, egos, beliefs, whatever. To forget this could ultimately affect the very nature of your institution. In other words, institutions are only as strong and effective as the people who represent them.

Craig Ross

Institution-Building

*"Institution-builders leave a legacy that transcends them."—**Steve A. Champion and Craig A. Ross***

We've spent many years communicating with gang members about what steps they need to take to transform their lives. One of the most important steps in the transformative process for Crips and Bloods is the creation of an institute that addresses their fundamental problems. We're talking about areas such as, but not limited to, gang violence, conflict resolution, job creation, and education. An institute organizes, enhances, and harnesses the energy and potential of people to achieve goals and sustainable change.

An institution can be defined as a group of people with a common purpose, a common discipline, and common goals. There are institutions of all kinds and sizes: churches, colleges, banks, foundations, military academies, think tanks, and international organizations such as the Boy Scouts and the Red Cross. Anyone seeking to start an institution needs to pose two basic questions:

1) What kind of institute do we need?
2) What performance is expected of it?

While there are institutions that involve all kinds of organized human activity, we focus here on both non-profit and micro-institutions with a social purpose.

As African Americans, creating organizations is part of our legacy. Each generation of African Americans have continued to build upon and add to this rich and diverse legacy that includes churches, schools, foundations, banks, and museums, newspapers, philanthropic organizations, insurance companies, movie studios, and more. It is important to study our history to learn how our people achieved what that they have. The models are there.

African Americans first created institutions in the United States in the eighteenth century in the form of independent black Baptist Churches in the South, especially in Georgia and Virginia. Andrew Byran founded one of the first independent black churches in Savannah, Georgia. These independent black churches sprang up before the War of Independence, before there was a U.S. Constitution, while most African Americans were being held in legal slavery.

This trend continued through the 18th, 19th and 20th centuries. For more examples see below.

1787	Richard Allen and others formed the African Society of Philadelphia, which later became the African Methodist Episcopal Church.
1787	Prince Hall created the African Masonic Lodge Number 1.
1841	The New York Association for Political Education and Improvement of People of Color
1852	The League of Freedom (Boston)
1856	The Liberty Association (Chicago)

1881	Booker T. Washington created The Tuskegee Institute
1900s	The African Educational Society
1914	Marcus Garvey formed the Universal Negro Improvement Association
1925	The Noble Drew Ali set up The Moorish Science Temple
1930	The Honorable Fard Muhammad started the Nation of Islam
1935	Mary McLeod Bethune created the Council for Negro Women
1964	Malcolm X began the Organization of Afro-American Unity
1966	Huey P. Newton and Bobby Seale started the Black Panther Party
1979	Ivan Van Sertima set up the Journal of African Civilizations
1982	Mary Carter Smith and Linda Goss founded the National Association of Black Storytellers (NABS)
2004	Geoffrey Canada created the Promise Academy in the Bronx
2007	Oprah Winfrey created and financed a leadership academy for South Africa girls

No institution is created out of thin air. They are created by individuals who see a need for it. Booker T. Washington exemplifies this best. He understood how important it was for African Americans to become self-reliant. He created the Tuskegee Institute, which not only provided academic opportunities but also an array of vocational skills. Every building built on the Tuskegee campus was built by its students. Due to Washington's vision and ideas, this institution still stands today, attracting students from all around the world. [1]

Look around any neighborhood where gang violence is constant and ask yourself, "Where are the institutions to address the problems?" And more importantly, "Why haven't gang members created or developed an institute that would help them and their neighborhoods?" The need is definitely there, but where is the vision, initiative, will, and creativity?

The biggest challenge of a purpose-driven organization is to meet expectations, not only of its members, but also of the community in which

---

[1] It's important we distinguish between the founding and enormous historical value of the Tuskegee Institute and the infamous and horrible Tuskegee Experiments that took place much later.

it exists. An organization doesn't necessarily start with a fancy, decorative building. A building is simply the physical structure of the institution, just as a bulb is the glass encasement for the filament that creates the light.

Institution-building begins with people. It starts with an idea, and in many cases with the initiative of a single person. This person will have the strength of character and skill to bring and hold people together, as they work to build the organization up and guide it as all involved advance its ideas, philosophy, and mission. Consider, for a model, what Nelson Mandela and his African National Congress achieved!

The strongest, most effective institutions are those with adaptable structures that adjust to changing conditions in society. Institutions that practice this will often outlive the person(s) who created them, just as the national Council for Negro Women, created by Mary McLeod Bethune, outlived her and sustains her vision.

No one approach, like job creation, is a panacea to solve the social problems in gang-plagued neighborhoods. Yes, jobs would be a start, but the problems are multi-layered and require a multi-layered approach. A good start would be creating micro-institutions—smaller versions of a larger institution. They can be started almost anywhere—in a basement, in a living room, a den, a backyard, a garage: any place where people can talk in private.

Let's say two or three people decided to meet in a basement on a weekly basis to share ideas, debate, and discuss what's happening in their neighborhood. They begin formulating plans and strategies on how to improve their hood.

Such meetings might well lead to the formation of a micro-institute. They could also function as a study group and roundtable where ideas are explored, exchanged, and developed, not unlike what is seen every Sunday morning on talk shows such as *Meet the Press*—where panels of journalists, policy makers and other pundits discuss current political, social, and global issues. The way they exchange opinions and ideas would work to build a micro-institute.

Micro-institutes are naturally flexible and take many forms.

- A business-oriented micro-institute might focus on teaching and training people in financial management, economics, entrepreneurship, and small business start-up.

- A politically oriented micro-institute might offer political education classes, as did the

Black Panther Party, where knowledge of local, state, and national politics is shared.

• A leadership micro-institute might study leadership and help members acquire leadership skills.

People in every neighborhood could set up their own micro-institute and tailor it to address issues important to them. As a micro-institute attracts members and grows, the leaders may need to secure a building to accommodate the growth. Such a building might also serve as an incubator for related micro-institutes, which, taken together, could ultimately form a larger organization serving various needs in the community.

Whether you create a business, political, or leadership micro-institute, it must include social transformation as a primary goal. Take the Nation of Islam (NOI) as an example. Under the leadership of the Honorable Elijah Muhammad, the NOI took in gangsters, pimps, players, hustlers, prostitutes, drug addicts, ex-cons, and anti-social individuals that society had written off as irredeemable and lost. The NOI transformed their lives.

If the NOI and its social program hadn't been created, there wouldn't have been a

Malcolm X, Muhammad Ali, Minister Farakhan, Naim Akbar, and countless other men and women who were reformed and transformed by this organization.

If a group is going to have longevity and empower people, it requires committed and disciplined leaders who are institution-builders. These leaders must be able to create an environment for roundtable discussion aimed at solving the fundamental problems in the community and building networks to disseminate these ideas. The people are the institution, and the institution is only as good as its leadership.

When we reflect on the kind of institutions and organizations that could have impacted us and made a difference in our lives, we think of the Red Cross in its humanitarian aspects; the NOI with its social, economic, transformative programs; and the Blank Panther Party with its strong community service component. Institutions and/or organization that are proactively engaged in the social, economic and political affairs of the communities they exist in: these are what we envision Crips and Bloods gang members developing in their neighborhoods.

Hey Homie

When I was young, I took great pride in the fact that I was a Crip and represented my hood. For me, and most of my generation, it was about the real feeling of brotherhood we shared. That no matter what set we were from we were all part of a greater collective, which was Crip. This had a profound impact on me. I understood intuitively that our unity is what gave us potential.

This vision is still true today but internal conflict dominates our relationships. Instead of homeboys truly working together for a bigger purpose and common goals we cling to old grudges and revenge. We've moved away from the principles of unity; in fact unity has become a bad word, as if it's something negative. I can tell you that it is not. Unity is power— the power to create and build whatever we envisage. We need collective thinking and collective effort. We need unity if great change is going to happen in our neighborhood, in our communities.

Collectivity is one piece of something larger, but unless you see it, you won't be able to see the bigger picture. I want to leave you with this African proverb: If you want to go fast go alone, If you want to go far – go together. Homie, you have the power to decide if you want to go fast or if you want to go far.

Steve Champion

Collectivity

*"One for all and all for one!"—**Alexandre Dumas***

The term "collectivity" describes the principle of "collective cooperation," in which a group of individuals or organizations come together to build a strong union to work toward common objectives.

Collectivity is a natural human trait. People progress much more effectively when functioning as a unified group. Collectivity requires people to transcend individualism and commit their efforts to the creation and development of a system that becomes self-organizing and self-perpetuating.

Organizations like Mothers Against Drunk Driving (MADD) and The Coalition to End the Death Penalty are two groups that exemplify collectivity. Other examples where we see collectivity at work include missionary religious groups and NGOs (Non-Governmental Organizations) formed to help people in need around the world.

The concept of collectivity is certainly not a new one. People working together, with a shared purpose, are more powerful than isolated individuals. History shows us the devastating consequences when collectivity is absent or weak: sectarian (tribal) conflict, divide and conquer politics, extreme individualism, economic stagnation, and civil war. These consequences lead to apathy, distrust, disillusionment, and the breakdown of cohesion amongst people. We share some other historical examples of collectivity in Appendix E.

When people are seeking to build a movement, an institution, an organization, or a nation, they usually rely on the principles of collective action. Without this common collective consciousness, it is nothing more than fantasy to speak of having any kind of movement or organization with positive change as one of its main objectives.

Why Is Collectivity Necessary?

Given the reality of the prevailing problems witnessed daily in poor communities across the U.S., collectivity is needed to combine the strategies, methodologies, and resources of people and organizations fighting for positive change: safe neighborhoods, economic growth, and social unity.

The family is the oldest of all social institutions that practice the principles of collectivity. It is within this structure, when it is working, that we learn about collective effort and work, and this helps prepare us for the larger social framework.

If the family is dysfunctional or non-existent, children will obviously have a difficult time adapting to, or cooperating within, other social structures. At the same time, in the spirit of unity, we must recognize and respect different family dynamics.

One of the missions of collectivity is to focus on rebuilding family cohesion and strengthening family values. The social construct of family values is always a hot political topic during a presidential election. There is no shortage of political pundits or groups ready to define "the family." Family values differ within each family but most people agree on two points:

- The family structure in urban areas has been deteriorating for many years for many complex reasons.
- The "family unit," however it is defined, must be placed at the center of any social agenda for change and empowerment.

People must also recognize the multi-ethnic, multi-cultural, and multi-generational make-up of our neighborhoods and communities. Some of the obstacles that prohibit acceptance of this fact include ignorance, bias, and fear of change. But the principle of collectivity respects and embraces the diversity of our shared world. Unless we view humanity through a positive lens, we will never be able to fulfil the principle of collectivity, nor employ all its potential.

Collectivity incorporates a wide spectrum of elements and people that help to strengthen the foundation of unity; it organizes the energies, skills, talents, intellect, determination, and technologies of a people to ensure their advancement and success. We must recognize, respect, and *combine* different strategies, methodologies, and resources when it comes to fighting for broader social change. This is what makes collectivity both necessary and urgent.

How Is Collectivity Achieved?

Some individuals will try to oppose the building of collectivity. Their antagonistic attitudes and rhetoric toward collectivity come from their need for personal gain and individual power. They include politicians, religious figures, and gang members.

We know Crips and Bloods who resist collectivity and reject transforming themselves and their neighborhoods—not because it isn't the right thing to do or because collective action would not benefit them. They reject collectivity out of suspicion, fear of change, and fear of losing influence and power within their own group. The sad fact is that these "rejectionists" offer no vision or agenda of their own, only criticism.

To achieve the spirit of collectivity people must be emotionally and psychologically inspired by strong examples and tangible results—win the minds of the people, so to speak. Three steps are essential to achieve this.

- Step one requires a serious critique of the ongoing crisis of community leadership. When a movement, institute, or nation loses its direction and effectiveness in serving its people, it is due to a failure in leadership.

- Step two requires leaders to be both visionary and pragmatic enough to forge a synthesis of ideas that will institutionalize collectivity as their model. It also means commitment to an arduous struggle that won't be won overnight.

- Step three requires utilizing all the ideas put forth in *The Architect*.

Individualism doesn't build nations, organizations, and institutions, or produce social change and political empowerment. These things can only be accomplished by people working together. The saying "We progress, or we fail!" isn't just an old saying that reminds us of the need for diligent effort and a sense of urgency. In its emphasis on the collective "we," it is a prophetic truth.

START A LOCAL NONPROFIT AND HELP YOUR COMMUNITY

Nonprofits are organizations that don't have profit as their main motivation. Some can be described as charities, like the American Red Cross. There are taxation laws that cover the activities of nonprofits.

If you want to set one up—to improve collectivity by helping people meet the hood's need for amateur sport, gardening, a foodbank or something else, your new organization will have to obey the nonprofit laws. These are the steps to follow:

- *Register with the state. Nonprofits must register with their state to legally do business as a nonprofit corporation.*
- *Apply to the IRS for nonprofit status.*
- *Before starting activities to raise money, register by completing Form 1023: https://www.irs.gov/forms-pubs/about-form-1023*
- *Convene a Board – people to work with you on the nonprofit's activities.*
- *Write bylaws – how you and the others will make decisions and carry out plans.*

PART VII:
LEADERSHIP

Homeboy

I'm gonna tell you the realest truth you've probably never heard, but then again, you've probably already figured it out: there are many OGs who are idiots and don't deserve your respect or recognition, and all OGs aren't leaders and some leaders aren't OGs. This fact leads to the question: What defines leadership? I'll give you the short version because, really Homie, it ain't that complex.

Leadership is not about age, or who someone knows or is related to. If this is what you thought then you can chuck that shit out the window right now. Leadership is about character, training and vision. Leaders don't make up stuff as they go along, or just react to situations as they come up. Good leaders will always have a plan. They ensure that everyone around them understands the purpose of their mission, even when people don't fully grasp the vision. The best kind of leaders try to avoid being selfish. They make decisions in the best interest of everyone, not just themselves. Their actions show how to take responsibility and be accountable. This is what I think of as leadership, Homie.

Craig Ross

Defining Leadership

"Foresight is the lead that the leader has. Once he loses this lead and events start to force his hand, he is leader in name only."—**Robert K. Greenleaf**

The earliest written principles of leadership are found in ancient Egypt in the Instruction of Ptahhotep, circa 2300 BCE. Later, as civilization developed in countries like China, Greece, and Rome, writings about leadership and leaders evolved. Nations, societies, and organizations have thrived, fallen, or failed due to strong or weak leaders and leadership.

There are several possible ways to define leadership. Several definitions, concepts, and categories of leaders and leadership range from intellectual leaders who are devoted to ideas, knowledge and values, to inspirational leaders who motivate and inspire followers, to ideological leaders who are devoted to explicit goals and social change. They are all necessary and serve a valuable purpose. Our study of leadership has led us to conclude two things: (1) Leaders are agents of change; and (2) Leaders have the ability to influence and move their followers in a shared direction.

We know that leadership is not only defined by the ability to influence and obtain followers, but also by a leader's ability to empower and develop people's potential. Leadership is developing a vision, a portrait of the future that inspires and excites followers.

Huey P. Newton and Bobby Seale, for example, created a vision for social justice in the Black Panther Party. Their vision was clearly outlined in the Ten Point Program. Those who joined the party knew exactly what the vision was just by reading this program. A vision is a dream rooted in the needs of the people. It informs them where they are going, and leadership shows them how to get there.

Leaders transform followers into self-empowering leaders, so they become agents of change themselves. This happens in successful corporations, organizations, and social movements. The Honorable Elijah Muhammad developed a generation of leaders, most notably Malcolm X, who was transformed into a self-empowered leader and went on to become a change agent. The following diagram suggests different types of leadership:

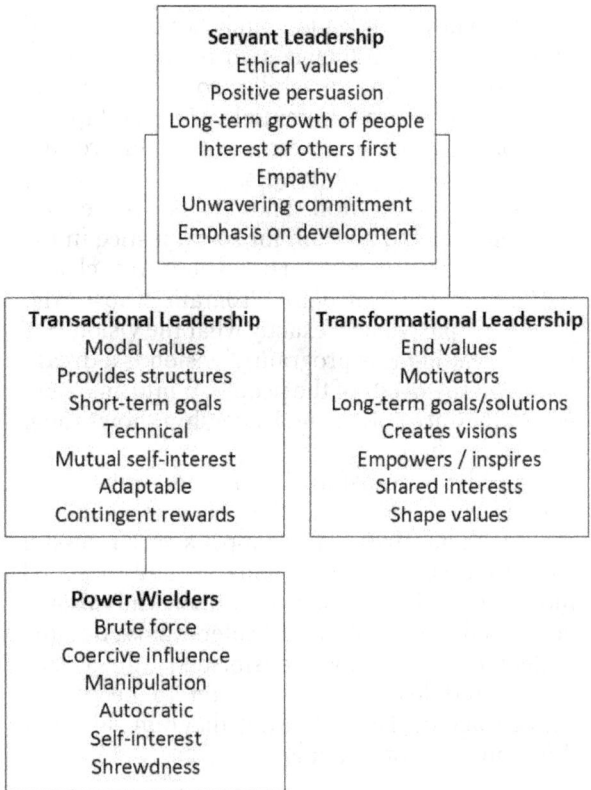

Servant Leadership
Ethical values
Positive persuasion
Long-term growth of people
Interest of others first
Empathy
Unwavering commitment
Emphasis on development

Transactional Leadership
Modal values
Provides structures
Short-term goals
Technical
Mutual self-interest
Adaptable
Contingent rewards

Transformational Leadership
End values
Motivators
Long-term goals/solutions
Creates visions
Empowers / inspires
Shared interests
Shape values

Power Wielders
Brute force
Coercive influence
Manipulation
Autocratic
Self-interest
Shrewdness

Hierarchical Structure Of Leadership

In the previous diagram, we outline the fundamental characteristics of each type of leadership. The sections below give a fuller picture. This is to inspire those seeking to be leaders – so they understand the kind of leader they aspire to become, and the kind they choose to avoid.

Power-Wielders

In the broader definition of leadership, power-wielders are gang leaders, war and/or drug lords, crime bosses, and tyrants. They don't lead, they rule. Their rule is autocratically enforced by strict, but simple codes of discipline and control, and through coercion, brute force, deceit, manipulation, and intimidation. The power-wielder has the capacity to solve problems, achieve goals, and organize resources. Unlike servant-leaders, transformational leaders, and transactional leaders, however, power-wielders don't have a moral imperative to transform their followers into change agents.

The personality of the power-wielder is driven by a selfish egotism that feeds on recognition and the desire to be in control. Thus, they are supreme over the followers, the law, and criticism.

Power-wielders don't see the need for a vision because all their goals are situational and subject to whim. They are adept at exploiting the wants and needs of people by creating false hope and short-term personal gain. Although power-wielders sometimes become transactional leaders, often they do not because they find the journey too arduous.

Transactional Leaders

Transactional leadership is very pragmatic. It is about the exchange between leaders and followers aimed at fulfilling both parties' self-interest. There is nothing of a higher purpose or mutual benefit that binds them. To succeed, this kind of leadership must operate on *moral values* of honesty, fairness, trust, commitment, and accountability. While transactional relationships aren't always trusting or solid, most leader-follower dynamics are transactional.

Being a transactional leader requires a shrewd eye for opportunity, skill at deal-making, power of persuasion, and the ability to bring conflicting sides to the bargaining table. But transactional leaders are not effective leaders in long-term planning because they have an "if it ain't broke, don't fix it" approach to leadership.

Thus, leaders must enhance their skills at leadership by incorporating aspects of both transactional and transformational leadership. Doing this develops leaders with the creative intelligence and intuitive grasp to meet the challenges of changing environments, and consequently to be effective and successful.

Transformational Leaders

Transformational leadership operates on *end values*: justice, equality, liberty, and collective benefit. Thus, transformational leaders are concerned with elevating their followers through levels of training. They recognize the followers' potential and qualities and emphasize personal development and empowerment. This nurturing relationship creates an exchange of mutual stimulation that transforms the follower into a leader and, in our view, an Architect of change.

Transformational leaders seek to motivate followers to have self-confidence and not to be afraid to pursue goals they may believe are impossible. They orient followers to plan long-term goals and solutions and inspire them to have a higher standard by transcending their own self-interest and taking responsibility for their commitments.

Two of the primary traits of transformational leaders are that they 1) create visions and 2) empower change. They are not merely going to preach to the choir; they are going to share and align their interest with the followers and act with conviction and purpose. This is what makes them more effective than transactional leaders and allows them to better cope with crises, adversity, conflict, and change. They are able to see and relate to the viewpoint of their followers.

Servant Leaders

According to Robert Greenleaf (author of *The Servant as Leader*), a servant-leader is "one who is servant first." This begins with a natural feeling that one's purpose is to serve, and the aspiration to lead follows as a conscious choice.

It is this primary characteristic—service—that puts servant-leaders at the top of the leadership hierarchy. The guiding principle of servant-leadership is ethical behavior and a deep commitment to followers and the vision. Servant-leaders will always return to the fundamental wants, needs, goals, and values of the followers. They form a symbiotic relationship with followers that binds them together into a collectivity of purpose and community. Like transformational leaders, servant-leaders emphasize the personal development and empowerment of followers.

Real Leadership

Real leadership is not merely symbolic or ceremonial. It is the moral and ethical vehicle for achieving and continuing a righteous purpose. Leadership must begin with a vision that can be translated into ideas and a blueprint. When leaders make decisions based on the best interest of others and from ethical values, they nullify the Machiavellian motive. Far too often people want to lead without the benefit of training and knowledge about what real leadership requires. As long as people fail to distinguish real leadership from power-wielders, a crisis in leadership will continue.

According to professor of political science James MacGregor Burns, "The most lasting tangible act of true leaders is the creation of an institution, a social movement, a political party, or an organization / foundation, that continues to perpetuate moral leadership and fosters social change long after the leaders are gone."

The Need for Ethical Leadership

"It is always easier to fight for one's principles than to live up to them."—Alfred Adler

To my Homie

What do you know about ethics, and how important it is to have them? I can tell you this: without ethics, the end justifies the means. Without ethical leadership, everyone is functioning according to however they are feeling in the moment because there is no real accountability. How many times have you seen one person drag everybody else into their mess when they were in the wrong but nobody held them accountable.

Ethics is the set of values that lay out how you should behave. It sets the standards for your actions. Ethical leadership holds everyone to the same standards. When you look at your OGs you want to be able to say, "these are leaders I want to follow." If you don't think this, then they are doing something wrong. Their ethics don't live up to the values you're looking for.

Ethical leadership is something you can respect and admire because it inspires and motivates you be at your best. This is what I want for you and all homies everywhere. I know that when you're at your best, this will create the new mindset. The next chapter "the need for ethical leadership" is just one part of a bigger picture. Take a look, see if you see it.

Steve Champion

As former gang members we know that an ethical value system is almost non-existent within gangs. Ethics have to be rooted in empathy, compassion, fairness and justice, and these values don't coexist well with the violent impetus that is the paradigm of gang life. Although we do recognize that gang members function with their own set of values, we also know that they are subject to distortion because of situational forces that have a direct effect on them. When personal values are connected to an idea of "being down," there will always be an inconsistency and contradiction between what you say and what you do.

In gang culture, "being down" loosely implies qualities such as character, integrity, loyalty, trust and commitment, but it is easy for these to be wrongly interpreted or not practiced at all because everybody can formulate their own opinion and definition as to what "being down" means. Adopting an ethical value system creates the first step towards correcting this problem.

Ethics should reflect the principles of right and wrong. It is precisely for this reason why having personal values is so important. Ethics gives you the means to make right choices and decisions for yourself. In every sphere of life—including business, education, politics, law, medicine, and military—there is a code of ethics that have the power to change the old "business as usual" approach. You need to demand viable solutions from your leaders, solutions that will make prison, parole, and the grave obsolete as life possibilities. You don't have to live with the negative expectation of not having a future. We understand how hard it is to re-examine beliefs, but when beliefs fail us, then we have every right, as a matter of survival, to remake them or discard them altogether.

Having a concrete ethical value system supports a clear vision for positive change that can help heal the wounds of violence that afflict your neighborhoods, communities and families. An ethical value system is absolutely necessary for gang members who want to transform their notions of leadership and responsibility.

We believe ethical leadership must first and foremost lead by example. Leaders have to be consistent in their own actions. This is what builds credibility and trust and sets the standard for others. People learn from what they see.

Gang members can tell so many stories about how their homies have betrayed and exploited them; how they told them one thing but did another. These kinds of incidents have created a deep disillusionment to sermons on change. We understand this, and we understand why younger gang members have a distrust towards leadership in general.

Having said that, we know you cannot survive in your current state without ethical leadership. If these leaders don't exist in your neighborhoods, then learn how to become one yourself. Set a higher expectation for accountability and integrity for yourself. You don't have to wait for anyone to come along and magically fix things for you. Take responsibility and your own personal stand and live by a value system that promotes and honors the peace, health and prosperity of your communities.

There have been, and will continue to be, leaders and people in every quarter of life who have acted unethically. Having an ethical value system does not mean people are immune to unethical actions. Anyone can twist and violate a value system to serve questionable ends. A good example of this is how the laws and ethics within the Bible and Koran have been distorted and misinterpreted to justify acts of brutal violence and terrorism.

The same can be said about the feuds between different gangs. The reasons for many of these conflicts and killings have either been exaggerated, distorted, or lost in history. Yet, some gang members continue to promote revenge violence for questionable ends by using old feuds to fuel new ones. This cycle of "tit-for-tat" can only be broken when the choice to live by a new ethics becomes the common denominator.

What we're asking you to do is to take complete ownership of your life by holding yourself accountable to real values. Start talking about what can be done to address the problems in your neighborhoods. Take the initiative to work out some concrete ethics you will live by. If you can achieve these very basic things, you will begin to see the fruits of your efforts.

Being A Leader

"Time is neutral and does not change things. With courage and initiative, leaders change things."
—Jesse Jackson

To my Homie

"Treach, you got potential to be a leader." This is what a lot of older guys would tell me when I was growing up, but it was never explained to me just what that actually meant. There came no guidance or instructions regarding what I should do about it. I'm certain this has happened to you also. Someone, at some point in your life, has told you that you have leadership potential yet they never told you how to develop it. Well, I want to change that. I want to give you a basic definitition of the traits of leadership so

that you will have a clear understanding and can build upon that.

There are many differing opinions about the traits that leaders should have, but I believe that above all a leader must have integrity—mean what you say and do what you say, and others will be inspired by your actions. In this chapter we list 9 core traits, that you should work on developing within yourself. These will strengthen your character. When we were writing this chapter, we literally had you in mind because we have witnessed too many potential leaders in our neighborhoods become lost to prison or the graveyard. We know that if we can build real leaders in our neighborhoods then we have a real chance at solving some of the major problems in our communities.

Honestly, you can't afford to waste time anymore. Our communities are in critical condition. You need to act now. You need to be the change you want to see in your neighborhood. Our communities need the best from you, and everyone like you, in order to survive and thrive.

Steve Champion

Traits of Leadership

Who would want to follow someone who is incompetent, irresponsible, or who lacks good judgment? No one would, but the signs of weak leadership are not always clear. Nonetheless, strong leaders share some identifiable traits, and we'd like to identify nine we call "the core nine." These traits must be developed in order for a leader to achieve maturity.

- **Integrity**: When words and actions match. Without integrity, leaders lose their credibility.
- **Responsibility**: Following through as well as owning up to mistakes. Without responsibility, leaders are not dependable or accountable.
- **Self-confidence**: Belief in Self. Leaders need faith in their own ability in order to take risks and complete tasks.
- **Self-discipline**: Reasonable control over one's mind and body. Leaders must master the Self to function at their maximum potential.
- **Judgment**: The ability to make sound, rational decisions based on all the available facts. Leaders must cultivate good judgment for the sake of all.
- **Ambition**: The desire to excel, succeed, and win: without it, leaders can become stagnant and regressive.
- **Conviction**: Adherence to sound principles. Gives leaders not only inner strength but the moral and intellectual fortitude to stay the course.

144

- **Humility**: Keeping the ego in check. When leaders are humble, they practice moderation in all areas of life.
- **Knowledge**: Always learning. Without acquiring knowledge, leaders cannot grow or move forward.

These nine core attributes may or may not occur simultaneously, or in any particular order, but leaders at some point must strive to embody each of them. Other important personal attributes include adaptability, initiative, persistence, intuition, insight, foresight, social intelligence, and critical thinking (both practical and creative). Even a sense of humor is known to relieve stress and improve morale.

Every organization that wants to be successful must have strong and intelligent leaders. For historical examples of effective leadership, see Appendix C.

The Choice Is Yours

As Crips and Bloods, you are faced with so many complex problems: violence against each other, disunity, the lack of education, the lack of an agenda, and the high incarceration rate. The first thing you must do is start with yourself. Do some serious soul searching and honest thinking, and then begin to formulate ideas about what actions to take. Ask yourself, "What am I doing to change this? How can I better myself?" As an active gang member, what do you stand for? This is one of the fundamental problems you must address: defining who you are, what you represent, and what will be your future mission. Unless you critically answer these questions, no real progress is going to be made and no real agenda can be mapped out. Ultimately, the choice is yours...

Courage

Be courageous and . . .
> Have the courage to do what is right.
> Have the courage to point out what is wrong.
> Have the courage to take a stance.
> Have the courage to pick yourself up
> > if you fall.
> Have the courage to be decisive.
> Have the courage to be fearless.
> Have the courage to make sacrifices.
> Have the courage to be humble.
> Have the courage to be compassionate.
> Have the courage to empathize.
> Have the courage to admit your faults.
> Have the courage to be patient.
> Have the courage to be committed.
> Have the courage to have new experiences.
> Have the courage to heal.
> Have the courage to forgive.
> Have the courage to seek understanding.
> Have the courage to learn knowledge.
> Have the courage to make a change.
> Have the courage to be yourself.
> Have the courage to believe in yourself.
> Have the courage to be great.
> Have the courage to be an Architect.

Steve Champion & Craig Ross

App A:
The Inescapability of Politics

Ross: So, what does it mean to become politically aware?

Champion: Basically, it means waking up and understanding the problems in your community and learning how to influence the political process to bring about the change you want. We know of many former and active gang members who are now politically active and have started organizations aimed at bringing about positive change in their hoods, and some of them are having real success. Making a shift from gang violence to political and social action doesn't mean you are not staying true to yourself. It just means you are smart enough to look at all of your options, in what seems like a no-win situation, for creating a better environment for your neighborhood.

Ross: I don't think it's an overstatement to say that whether or not gang members remain a permanent fixture on the revolving door of incarceration literally depends on their political, social, and economic transformation. This transformation is going to require a new kind of thinking and direction that begins with getting *politically involved in organizing people at the grassroots level.*

Champion: *Yeah, without being organized and having a clear agenda, trying to impact political decisions at City Hall is like having a car without an engine. You won't get anywhere. But when you are organized into a political bloc, then can you exercise political influence. And a political bloc is simply a group of people or businesses united for a common purpose. For instance, what if the City Council decides to rezone areas in your neighborhood for toxic waste disposal or new freeways, or pass an ordinance that limits the number of people in a group? What political influence will gang members have on these decisions? None at all, if they aren't politically organized. The logic is simple: if you are concerned about the politics that affect your life, then you can't complain about any changes City Hall dictates in your neighborhood. To have a voice, to make an impact politically, you have to be actively involved in the most important drama of your life — politics.*

Ross: *We know that all gang members are not on the same page when it comes to looking at the bigger picture. But most gang members have something in common no matter their age or* *where they're from, and that's a love for their hood—wanting his or her neighborhood to be a safe place to live, work, go to school, and grow up in. It's this love for the hood that has to be channeled into political action for change that's positive and remarkable. This is the strongest tool gang members have for transforming their hood and themselves.*

Champion: *I know a lot of people think gang members and political action may appear paradoxical, but it is not a new idea. In the mid-1960s, many Los Angeles gang members became politically active. In the early 1990s, gang members in Chicago formed a neighborhood political organization and encouraged voter registration and supported local candidates for political office. By the early 2000s, all across the country gang members were starting their own neighborhood organizations that tackled an array of social issues. Some of these organizations failed due to a lack of leadership and vision, but others continue to grow. The examples are out there.*

Ross: *There's no law preventing gang members from becoming politically active. What gang members have to get over is their feeling of powerlessness — that they can't do anything* about the political changes happening all around them, especially if they have lost the right to vote because of a felony conviction. But not having the right to vote doesn't bar anyone from engaging in political action. You can still organize, speak, build networks, and attend City Hall meetings. You can still start neighborhood action committees, political education classes, and be part of political protest. Not having the right to vote is no excuse for not being politically active in your neighborhood.

Champion: We can look at the Black Lives Matter movement and see how it has galvanized so many people to become politically involved, not just around the issue of police officers murdering unarmed black men and women, but also around other important systemic social problems in black and poor communities. Gang members can no longer afford to continue to be politically passive and ignore the political reality around them. Ignorance is not bliss in this case: it's dangerous.

Ross: We read, hear, and see in the news every day tragic stories about people losing their lives to gang violence. This is the ugly cycle our communities have had to live with for decades. And it is this very gang violence that reduces one generation after the other to political invisibility. The question is not, why should gang members become politically active? The question is, why not? Who protects your most basic rights when you can't speak or stand up for yourself?

Champion: *Coming from the gang life, we know gang members don't have political experience, so they lack the background for understanding the importance of thinking politically. This is why, in the very Neighborhood Council meetings addressing gang violence, gang members themselves are conspicuously absent. They don't think of themselves as part of the solution, nor are they invited into the decision-making process. Getting gang members to commit to fundamental changes must go hand-in-hand with having the experience of being able to solve problems in their neighborhoods.*

Ross: *Politics is one of the ways to change and control your destiny. What political action can give you is political power to impact public policy and decide who gets into public office. Having political strategies that expand beyond just resolving gang violence to combating poverty, illiteracy, substance abuse, homelessness, policing reforms, etc. means your* *community, your neighborhood, and yourselves become a powerful collective voice with genuine political objectives.*

Champion: *Gang members have to be willing to make real sacrifices to reap real benefits from their actions, and political action is a road to self-sufficiency and having a future that truly matters. Being a part of the change in your neighborhood, seeing the community transformed because of your contributions, should be a great source of pride and dignity for everyone.*

APP B:
EXPLORING MAATIAN ETHICS

*"The ancient Egyptian symbol for precision is the
feather that is used to weigh souls against. The
Maat, as well as being the feather, was also the
standard measurement of a brick and the
fundamental note of the flute."— **Italo Calvino***

Ethics (and the need for them) have been a topic
of philosophical discussion for over five thousand
years, so the theories on ethics and ethical
leadership are diverse and vast. The first known
ethical system was the Ancient Egyptian Maat
ethics and the oldest known book on ethics was
the "Book of Instruction on Ethics" by Ptahhotep
(c.2350-2310 BCE).

Maat is an Egyptian word with both social
and cosmological significance as explained in the
chapter on Maat, Brotherhood and Sisterhood
(within PART IV on Fraternity). Maat means
Truth, Justice, Righteousness, Order, Reciprocity
and Harmony. In his book *Odu If a: The Ethical
Teachings*, the scholar and intellectual Maulana
Karenga outlines four fundamental pillars of
African ethical tradition consistent with Maat: 1)
the dignity and rights of the human person; 2) the
well-being and flourishing of the family and

community; 3) the integrity and value of the environment; and 4) the reciprocal solidarity and common interest of humanity. Constituting the cosmic, natural, and social order of that nation, Maat was a fundamental imperative in ancient Khemetian society. The essence and cosmic aspect of Maat has its beginnings with the creator itself.

The ethics of Maat can to be utilized to build a strong social order and moral culture within brotherhood and sisterhood, just as it once was used to build a strong Khemetian nation. In the ancient Egyptian *Book of Ani* (circa 1250 BCE), people are advised to "Walk each day in the way of righteousness and you will reach the place you're going."

Ani's statement prescribes what brotherhood and sisterhood ought to strive for. The idea to walk each day in the way of righteousness requires a daily (or regular) ritual or practice, and self-conscious effort, to live a righteous life. With such effort, Maat is maintained.

Another Saba (moral teacher), Ptah Hotep, who was vizier of King Isesi in the fifth dynasty (circa 2350 - 2310 BCE), had this to say: "If right exists in the heart of those who have been in authority, they will be beneficent always and their wisdom shall endure forever." We assert in the same vein, brotherhood and sisterhood based on Maat will endure.

There is a correlation between each virtue of Maat. Below we provide a working definition of each virtue along with quotes from spiritual teachers. The ethics of Maat are interlinked and overlapping: each one gives strength and credence to the other.

- **Truth**: As one saying goes, "When we hear the truth, we will recognize it because it will feel true inside us." Deepak Chopra says: "When you tell the truth, you speak to the truth in others. They may hide from their own truth, but you are seeking to free them, in the process making your truth stronger." Even though it can be painful, truth ultimately liberates us.

- **Justice**: This doesn't refer only to moral rightness or conformity to moral rightness in action or attitude. It's fairness. Fairness in one's dealings and actions. Brother Amon Re says, "The ability to give justice depends on our skill in ignoring fear and anger."

- **Righteousness**: This is the consistent practice of both truth and justice, which are the essence of Maat.

- **Harmony:** Just as different notes in a chord are in agreement with the whole, for humans, harmony represents unity in diversity. Manly P. Hall writes: "Before man can live together in harmony and understanding, ignorance must be transmuted into wisdom, supervision into an illuminated faith, and fear into love."

- **Order**: There's a divine order in the universe. Brother Amon Ra says: "Order is essentially dependent on existence of interdependence (oneness) between things." Without order and interdependence, humans could not survive as a species.

- **Reciprocity**: This refers to mutual cooperation. According to John, Jesus said: "Abide in me as I abide in you" (John 15:3-4), which teaches us in spiritual terms the unity we share with each other and the creator.

Through your own experience, you will know the truth. As counseled in the book of Ani: "Take them for a brother one who is true and just, one whose actions you have observed. And if your righteousness equals his or hers, your brotherhood will be balanced."

APP C:
THINKING ABOUT LEADERSHIP

The old axiom that if you ask five people to define something you will probably get five different answers is pertinent when it comes to defining leadership. In his book *Developing the Leader Within You,* John Maxwell writes, "Leadership is influence and the ability to obtain followers." One can debate Maxwell's definition and argue the moral implications involved, as history is surfeited with stark examples of leaders who were downright cruel and inhumane toward their own population and others. Unfortunately, being morally bankrupt, being tyrant or fool, doesn't prevent a person from leadership.

Effective leaders marry their vision with the values and aspirations of the people. Some excellent examples of this include the following: 1) The founding fathers of the United States of America. Regardless of one's personal views about them, they clearly had a vision of a republic and realized it by creating the Declaration of Independence and U.S. Constitution, documents that are the heart and soul of this country; 2) Joseph Smith claimed to have received visions from God. He acted on his vision by creating the Mormon Church of Latter-Day Saints; 3) Marcus

Garvey had a vision of uniting black people worldwide and created an organization, The Universal Negro Improvement Association, which became the largest black organization that has ever existed in the U.S.

It also happens in teacher/student relationships. The Buddha and Jesus both were teachers who taught, developed, and empowered their followers to became "change agents" and spread their message. Socrates was a teacher who trained and developed many students—the most famous of whom was Plato, who opened an academy and became a change agent. His ideas shaped and influenced Western civilization.

Danah Zohar (author of *Rewiring the Corporate Brain*) writes, "Servant-leadership is the essence of quantum thinking and quantum leadership." By "quantum" she means the ability to synthesize creativity, skills, knowledge, concepts, and ideas into a higher order of functioning. This is because servant-leadership's effectiveness and planning are measurable and visible, and servant-leaders consistently put the interests of the followers before their own, which exemplifies their fundamental character trait. Servant-leadership emphasizes emotional intelligence and empathy to nurture an attitude and temperament conducive to one's purpose and position. It can never be overstated how much we need servant-leaders. They have the ability to transcend linear thinking, to integrate new knowledge, qualitatively transform people, and create new paradigms.

The Prince by Niccolo Machiavelli is the best-known treatise on wielding power. Machiavelli proposes that one must become both the fox and the wolf in order to better manipulate and crush all opposition. This and other seemingly practical advice can only be practiced if one is willing to cultivate the worst within themselves. This means eliminating whatever values, principles, and humanity you have. What Machiavelli suggests in the twenty-six chapters of his book is that everyone should be treated like mere pawns, tools, and objects. This ideology of ruthlessness is the primary dictum of power-wielders.

One of the most lasting acts of leadership is to create an institution; however, in most gang neighborhoods we don't see this happening due to a lack of leadership. Robert Greenleaf, in his book *Servant Leadership*, writes, "An institution starts on a course toward people—building with leadership that has a firmly established context of people first." In other words, "people-building" comes first. And this requires putting into place a system that lifts people up, so they become wiser, stronger, more independent, and self-empowered. We need organizations that can create better people, better communities and, ultimately, a better society.

According to writer James MacGregor Burns, "An institution is but the lengthened shadow of a man (or woman), but it takes many men and women to establish lasting institutions." That is why every institution must continually revisit and reaffirm what it is about and not only when forced to because of a scandal or disaster.

In his book *Visions for Black Men*, Dr. Naim Akbar writes, "The only way you can operate equitably in a world like this is to have our institutions defining your own reality and engaging in a dialogue of human progress from your perspective. You've got to have it. Until you have it, you'll never get respect."

Being a leader is who you are, or who you become. Leadership is what you do and how you do it. No leader will ever define leadership; he or she can only exemplify it. But leadership, good or bad, will always define the leader.

The impact of effective leadership can be profound. But this can only happen, when the interest of the people is greater than the interest of the leader(s).

APP D:
THINKING ABOUT FRATERNITY

One of the qualities of fraternity is in understanding the real meaning of sacrifice. Joseph Campbell, the famous mythology scholar, writes, "When we quit thinking primarily about ourselves and our own self-preservation, we undergo a profound heroic transformation of consciousness." The willingness to give of ourselves without expecting anything in return exemplifies true altruism. Altruism is not about *giving up* something, it is about *giving*.

According to the Samurai code of Bushido, the selfless acts of one's brother are considered actions of the highest honor. A true brother does not ask himself what is in it for him or expect payment in kind for what is given. Such self-centeredness is completely absent in true fraternity.

There is an ancient story that perfectly illustrates the transcendent bonds of brotherhood. One day a brother of the Pythagorean Order became ill and fell into poverty. He was taken in by a kindly innkeeper who did his best to nurse the brother back to health. But unfortunately, the brother was too sick and unable to regain his strength. Before dying, he traced several symbols on the wall of the inn, telling the innkeeper, "Do not be worried, one of my brothers will pay my debt." Many years later, a stranger came to the inn and saw the symbols on the wall, telling the innkeeper, "One of my brothers died here. How much do I owe you?"

This story shows the extraordinary bond of fraternity and how it always aspires towards the highest virtues. It shows that true brotherhood is timeless because it exists on its own conditions and terms apart from external forces. Fraternity is its own consciousness, independent of any other influences.

APP E:

EXAMPLES OF COLLECTIVITY

According to historian Dr. John Henrik Clarke, the first historical record of collectivity can be traced as far back as 3200 BCE, when King Menes united the upper (Southern) and lower (Northern) kingdoms of ancient Khemet (later becoming Egypt). Menes has been recognized as the king who ushered in the first nation-state, uniting two lands and two peoples under the principle of collectivity.

History is replete with examples of collectivity, one of the more potent being the U.S. Civil War. Without going into an analysis of the causes of the Civil War, the basic issue that influenced President Abraham Lincoln's decision to go to war was saving the union. In an 1862 letter to Horace Greely, editor of the *New York Tribune*, Lincoln wrote, "If I could save the union without freeing a single slave, I would. If I have to free every slave to save the union, I would." We see clearly from Lincoln's own words how much importance he placed on unity. Chattel slavery was an abominable institution, but African Americans were secondary to Lincoln's strategy. Although Abolitionists like Fredrick Douglas and William Lloyd Garrison were pressing the president to end slavery, his primary concern was preserving the unified structure of the United States and stopping the succession by the southern states at any cost.

In 2011 and 2012, for instance, the Occupy movements, in which people came together around various issues, sprang up around the U.S. In Wisconsin, hundreds of people occupied the state capitol in protest of Governor Walker's elimination of the public workers' union's collective bargaining rights. And other Occupy movements around the country gained national media attention by occupying state buildings, parks, and public spaces. The many thousands of people represented the aptly named "99 Percent" of the population that was not benefiting from an economy and government controlled by corporations and greedy Wall Street banks. These Occupy movements successfully dramatized specific social ills and demonstrated the power of collectivity. Another good example of collective action is the successful amendment of California's destructive Three Strikes law by a host of activists, organizations, state legislators, and some law-enforcement agencies working together. Locally, people have been using collectivity to create urban gardens, build homes for low-income families, and start programs aimed at stopping violence and keeping neighborhoods safe.

SELECTED BIBLIOGRAPHY

We have compiled a general book list, and a list of books under various subjects. This list is in no way definitive or exhaustive. We hope each book will lead the reader to pursue other books, and most importantly, become inspired, enriched and enlightened.

General List
- Akbar, Na'im
  - *Know Thy Self*
  - *From Miseducation to Education*
  - *Vision for Black Men*
- Alexander, Michelle
  - *The New Jim Crow*
- Amen, Ra Un Nefer
  - *An Afrocentric Guide to a Spiritual Union*
  - *Tree of Life Meditation System*
- Armah, Ayi Kwei
  - *Two Thousands Seasons*
- Asante, Molefi Kete
  - *Afrocentricity*
  - *The Afrocentric Idea*
  - *Kemet, Afrocentricity and Knowledge*
- Becker, Konrad
  - *Tactical Reality Dictionary*

- Bell, Derrick
  - *And We Are Not Saved: The Elusive Quest for Racial Justice*
- Ben-Jochannan, Yosef
  - *Black Man of the Nile*
  - *African Origins of Major "Western Religions"*
- Blyden, Edward W.
  - *Christianity, Islam, and the Negro Race*
- Boggs, Grace Lee
  - *The Next American Revolution*
- Browder, Anthony T.
  - *From the Browder File Vol II: Survival Strategies for Africans in America: 13 Steps to Freedom*
- Brzezinki, Zbigniew
  - *Strategic Vision: America and the Crisis of Global Power*
- Butterfield, Fox
  - *All God's Children: The Bosket Family and the American Tradition of Violence*
- Carr, Williams
  - *Pawns in the Game*
  - *The Red Fog Over America*
- Carruthers, Jacob
  - *Essays in Ancient Egyptian Studies*
  - *Science and Oppression*
  - *Intellectual Warfare*

- Cesaire, Aime
  - *Discourse on Colonialism*
- Chomsky, Noam
  - *Understanding Power: The Indispensable Chomsky*
- Clarke, Henrik
  - *Africans at the Crossroads: African World Revolution*
- Cleary, Thomas
  - *Thunder in The Sky*
- Coates, Ta-Nehesi
  - *Between the World and Me*
- Cole, David
  - *No Equal Justice: Race and Class in the American Criminal Justice System*
- Cruse, Harold
  - *The Crisis of the Negro Intellectual: A Historical Analysis of the Failure of Black Leadership*
- Cumming, Eric
  - *The Rise and Fall of California's Radical Prison Movement*
- Davis, Angela
  - *The Prison Industrial Complex*
- DeGruy, Joy Angela
  - *Post Traumatic Slave Syndrome: America's Legacy of Enduring Injury and Healing*

- Diop, Cheikh Anta
  - *The African Origin of Civilization: Myth or Reality*
  - *Pre-Colonial Black Africa*
  - *Black Africa: The Economic and Cultural Basis for a Federated State*
  - *The Cultural Unity of Black Africa*
  - *Civilization or Barbarism: An Authentic Anthropology*
- Du Bois, W.E.B.
  - *The World and Africa*
  - *The Souls of Black Folk*
  - *Black Reconstruction in America*
  - *(Anything by Du Bois)*
- Epperson, Ralph
  - *The Unseen Hand: An Introduction to the Conspiratorial View of History*
- Fanon, Frantz
  - *The Wretched of the Earth*
  - *Black Skin, White Masks*
  - *A Dying Colonialism*
- Frazier, E. Franklin
  - *Black Bourgeoisie*
  - *The Negro Family in the United States (co-authored with Anthony Platt)*
- Garvey, Marcus G.
  - *The Philosophy and Opinions of Marcus Garvey, Or, Africa for the Africans*

- Gilbert, Jill
  - *The Entrepreneur's Guide to Patents, Copyrights, Trademarks, Trade Secrets, and Licensing*
- Gray, Chris
  - *Conceptions of History in the Works of Cheikh Anta Diop and Theophile Obenga*
- Haidt, Jonathan
  - *The Righteous Mind: Why Good People are Divided by Politics and Religion*
- Hilliard, Asa
  - *SBA: The Reawakening of the African Mind (co-authored with Wade W. Nobles)*
- Hare, Nathan & Julia
  - *The Endangered Black Family*
  - *Bringing the Black Boy to Manhood*
  - *Crisis in Black Sexual Politics (eds.)*
  - *Black Anglo-Saxons (Nathan Hare)*
- Jackson, John G.
  - *Man, God, and Civilization*
  - *Christianity Before Christ*
- Jackson, George L.
  - *Blood in My Eye*
- Karenga, Maulana
  - *Kwanzaa: A Celebration of Family, Community and Culture*
- Kinzer, Stephen

173

> *Garvey and the Universal Negro Improvement Association*

- Mullins, Eustace
  - *The Secrets of the Federal Reserve*
  - *The World Order: Our Secret Rulers*
- Nkrumah, Kwame
  - *Neo-Colonialism: The Last Stage of Imperialism*
- Nobles, Wade
  - *Africanity and the Black Family*
  - *Understanding the Black Family: A Guide for Scholarship and Research (with Lawford Goddard)*
  - *African-American Families: Issues, Insights and Directions* (with Goddard, Cavil and George)
- Obenga, Theophile
  - *Pre-Colonial Congo*
  - *Ancient Egypt & Black Africa*
- Padmore, George
  - *Pan-Africanism or Communism*
- Paretti, Michael
  - *Democracy for the Few*
- Perkins, John
  - *Economic Hitman*
- Perkins, Useni Eugene
  - *Harvesting New Generations*
- Rashidi, Runoko

- ➢ *Black Star: The African Presence in Early Europe*
- Rogers, J.A.
  - ➢ *Sex and Race, Vol. 1-3*
- Rubin, Alex
  - ➢ *Geographies of Liberation*
- Sanchez, Sonia
  - ➢ *Homegirls and Handgrenades*
- Toure, A.
  - ➢ *The African Intelligentsia in Timbuktu*
- Understanding, Supreme
  - ➢ *How to Hustle and Win*
- Van Sertima, Ivan
  - ➢ *They Came before Columbus: The African Presence in Ancient America (Journal of African Civilizations)*
  - ➢ *Blacks in Science: Ancient and Modern (Journal of African Civilizations)*
  - ➢ *Black Women in Antiquity (Journal of African Civilizations)*
  - ➢ *Great African Thinkers (Cheikh Anta Diop)*
  - ➢ *Great Black leaders Ancient and Modern (Journal of African Civilizations)*
  - ➢ *African Presence in Early Asia (with Runoko Rashidi)*
  - ➢ *African Presence in Early Europe (Journal of African Civilizations)*

- ➤ *(Anything in the Journal of African Civilization)*
- Ward, Churchill and Wall, James V.
  - ➤ *The Cointelpro Papers*
  - ➤ *Cages of Steel*
- Weatherford, J.
  - ➤ *Indian Giver*
- Web, Gary
  - ➤ *Dark Alliance*
- Wilhelm, Sidney M.
  - ➤ *Who Needs the Negro?*
- Williams, Chancellor
  - ➤ *The Rebirth of African Civilization*
  - ➤ *The Destruction of Black Civilization*
- Wilson, Amos
  - ➤ *The Developmental Psychology of the Black Child*
  - ➤ *Blueprint for Black Power*
  - ➤ *Black on Black Violence*
- Wilson, Julius
  - ➤ *The Truly Disadvantaged: The Inner City, the Underclass, and Public Policy*
- Woodson, Carter G.
  - ➤ *The Mis-Education of the Negro*
- Woodward, C.V.
  - ➤ *The Strange Career of Jim Crow*

Subject - Philosophy

- Aristotle
  - ➢ *On Heavens*
- Griaule, Marcel
  - ➢ *Philosophy and Black Religions*
- Heidegger, Martin
  - ➢ *Introduction to Metaphysics*
- James, G.M.
  - ➢ *Stolen Legacy*
- Kant, Immanuel
  - ➢ *The Critique of Pure Reason*
- Nkrumah, Kwame
  - ➢ *Consciencism*
- Obenga, Theophile
  - ➢ *African Philosophy – The Pharaonic Period: 2800 - 330 BC*
- Plato
  - ➢ *Plato's Republic*
- Sartre, Jean Paul
  - ➢ *Existentialism and Humanism*
- Wiredu, Kwasi
  - ➢ *Philosophy and African Culture*
- Wright, Richard
  - ➢ *African Philosophy: An Introduction*

Subject - Psychology

- Akbar, Naim
  - ➢ *Psychological Chains and Images*

- Ani, Marimba
  - *Yurugu: An African-Centered Critique of European Cultural Thought*
- Freud, Sigmund
  - *The Interpretation of Dreams*
- Fromm, Eric
  - *To Have or to Be?*
- Grier, W.H. & Cobbs, P.M.
  - *Black Rage*
- Jung, Carl
  - *Collected Works of C.G. Jung*
- Marcuse, Herbert
  - *Eros and Civilization: A Philosophical Inquiry into Freud*
- Poussaint, A.F. & Alexander, A.
  - *Lay My Burden Down: Suicide and the Mental Health Crisis Among African-Americans*
- Skinner, B.F.
  - *Verbal Behavior*
- Welsing, Frances Cress
  - *The Isis Papers*
- Wilson, Amos
  - *Falsification of African Consciousness*
- Wright, Bobby
  - *The Psychopathic Racial Personality*

Subject - Spirituality/Religion

- Allen, James
  - ➢ *As a Man Thinketh*
- Amen, Ra Un Nefer
  - ➢ *Metu Neter, Vol. 1 & 2*
- Budge, Wallis
  - ➢ *The Book of Coming Forth by Day*
- Campbell, Joseph
  - ➢ *The Power of Myth*
- Chopra, Deepak
  - ➢ *The Third Jesus*
- Cleary, Thomas
  - ➢ *Dhammapada: The Sayings of Buddha*
- Ford, Clyde W.
  - ➢ *The Hero with an African Face*
- Hall, Manly P.
  - ➢ *The Secret Teachings of All Ages*
- Lao Tzu
  - ➢ *The Way of Life: I Ching*
- Mbiti, John
  - ➢ *African Religions*
- Neimak, Philip J.
  - ➢ *The Way of Orisha: Empowering Your Life Through the Ancient African Religion of Ifa*
- Rama, Swami
  - ➢ *The Perennial Psychology of the Bhagavad Gita*

- Rinpoche, Sogyal
  - *The Tibetan Book of Living and Dying*
- Ross, Champion & Williams
  - *The Sacred Eye of the Falcon*
- Ruiz, Don Miguel
  - *The Four Agreements: A Toltec Wisdom Book*
- Somé, Malidoma
  - *Of Water and Spirit*
- Thurman, Robert
  - *Tibetan Book of the Dead*
- Trunpa, Chogypan
  - *The Sacred Path of the Warrior*
- Wilson Ross, Nancy
  - *Buddhism: A Way of Life and Thought*

Subject - Leadership
- Bass, Bernhard B.
  - *The Bass Handbook of Leadership*
- Bunting, Josiah
  - *Critical Lessons of Leadership: The Case for National Public Service*
- Cleary, Thomas
  - *Mastering the Art of War*
- DePree, Max
  - *Leadership is an Art*
- Greenleaf, Robert K.
  - *Servant leadership*

- ▸ *The Leader as a Servant*
- Hunter, James C.
  - ▸ *The Servant*
- Mac Gregor Burn, James
  - ▸ *Leadership*
- Maxwell, John
  - ▸ *Building the Leader Within*
- T'Shaka, Oba
  - ▸ *The Art of Leadership, Vol. 1 & 2*
- Willink, Jocko and Leif Babin
  - ▸ *Extreme Leadership: How the U.S. Navy SEALs Lead and Win*

Subject - African History for Beginners
- Browder, Anthony
  - ▸ *From the Browder File*
- Jackson, John
  - ▸ *Introduction to African History*
- Karenga, Maulana
  - ▸ *Introduction to Black Studies*
- Malcolm X
  - ▸ *Malcolm X on Afro-American History*
- Rogers, J.A.
  - ▸ *Great Man of Color, Vol. 1 & 2*
- Williams, Richard
  - ▸ *They Stole It But You Must Return It*

Subject - Slavery/Slave Trade

- Aptheker, Herbert
  - ➤ *American Negro Slave Revolts*
- Bennett, Lerone
  - ➤ *Before the Mayflower*
  - ➤ *The making of Black America*
- Blackmon, Douglas
  - ➤ *Slavery by Another Name*
- Carew, Jan
  - ➤ *Fulcrum of Change*
- Douglas, Frederick
  - ➤ *My Bondage, My Freedom*
  - ➤ *Narrative of the Life of F. Douglas*
- Goodell, W.
  - ➤ *The African Slave Code*
- Harding, Vincent
  - ➤ *There is a River*
- Hugh, Thomas
  - ➤ *The Slave Trade: The Story of the Atlantic Slave Trade, 1440-1870*
- Rodney, Walter
  - ➤ *How Europe Underdeveloped Africa*
- Stampp, K.
  - ➤ *The Peculiar Institution: Slavery in the Ante Bellum South*
- Washington, Booker T.
  - ➤ *Up from Slavery*
- Williams, Eric

> *Slavery and Capitalism*
- Zinn, Howard
  > *A People's History of the U.S.A.*

Subject - Autobiography/Memoirs
- Abu-Jamal, Mumia
  > *Live from Death Row*
- Belafonte, Harry
  > *My Song*
- Biko, Steve
  > *I Write What I Like*
- Black, Jack
  > *You Can't Win*
- Brown, Claude
  > *Manchild in the Promised Land*
- Brown, Elaine
  > *A Taste of Power*
- Champion, Steve
  > *Dead to Deliverance*
- Cleaver, Eldridge
  > *Soul on Ice*
- Davis, Angela
  > *If They Come in the Morning*
- Dubois, W.E.B.
  > *The Autobiography of W.E.B. Dubois*
- Hillard, David
  > *This Side of Glory*
- Malcolm X

-     ➢ *The Autobiography of Malcolm X*
- Mandela, Nelson
  - ➢ *The Struggle is My Life*
  - ➢ *Long Walks to Freedom*
- McBride, James
  - ➢ *The Color of Water*
- Masters, Jarvis
  - ➢ *That Bird Has My Wings*
- Nkrumah, Kwame
  - ➢ *Ghana: The Autobiography of Kwame Nkrumah*
- Obama, Barack
  - ➢ *Dreams of my Father*
- O'Hearn, Dennis
  - ➢ *But An Unfinished Song*
- Piri, Thomas
  - ➢ *Down these mean streets*
- Rice, Connie
  - ➢ *Power Concedes Nothing*
- Robinson, Randall
  - ➢ *Defending Spirit*
- Shukura, Assata
  - ➢ *Assata*
- Souljah, Sister
  - ➢ *No Disrespect*
- Williams, Tookie
  - ➢ *Blue Rage/Black Redemption*

AUTHOR BIOGRAPHIES

Steve Allen Champion

Steve Champion (also known as Adisa Akanni Kamara) is a death row prisoner at San Quentin State Prison. A Crip emeritus, from Raymond Avenue Crip, he grew up in South Central Los Angeles. Champion has been incarcerated for 37 years and counting. He is self-taught and conversant in African history, philosophy, political science, and comparative religion.

As an author he has received honorary mention in the short fiction category in the 1995 Pen Prison Writing Contest and in 2004 won first place in nonfiction for his essay, *His Spirit Lives On: George E. Marshall*. He is co-author of *Afterlife*, a death row anthology published in 2003, and he has poetry featured in the book *Voices From The Inside*. He is also co-author of several inspirational, self-help pamphlets, including *Walking It Like You Talk It, The Ninth Ground*, and *Everything Of Value You Must Carry Without Hands*.

His memorial poem for Stanley Tookie Williams, *My Brother is Gone*, was published early in 2006 on indybay.org and in other venues. In 2007 he co-authored *The Sacred Eye of the*

Falcon and in 2010 published a memoir titled *Dead to Deliverance*.

Steve continues to write and research for future projects. Send correspondence to:

Steve Champion
C-58001
San Quentin State Prison
San Quentin, California 94974

Craig Anthony Ross

Craig Anthony Ross (also known as Ajani Addae Kamara) was raised in South Central Los Angeles. A Crip emeritus, from Raymond Avenue Crip, Ross has been incarcerated for 37 years and counting. While in the hole—ten years in San Quentin's Adjustment Center—he began to study metaphysics, psychology, mythology, African and Asian history, and follow a spiritual path. He is now a recognized writer and mentor. In 1995 he won the Pen Prison Writing Award for best short fiction: *Walker's Requiem*, a riveting account of a young man's last day before being executed.

Craig has been published in several books and periodicals. He appears in the anthology *Children of the Dream: Growing Up Black in America*. He is co-author of several inspirational, self-help pamphlets, including *Walking It Like*

186

You Talk It, The Ninth Ground, and *Everything You Value You Must Carry Without Hands*. In 2007, he co-authored *The Sacred Eye of the Falcon*. Presently he is completing his memoir, *The Road to Purgatory*. His memorial prose poem for Stan Williams, *The Words Would Not Come,* also appeared on indybay.org and in other publications.

Craig continues to inspire others with his words. Send correspondence to:

Anthony Ross
C-58000
San Quentin State Prison
San Quentin, California 94974

Palewell Press

Palewell Press is an independent publisher
handling poetry, fiction and non-fiction with a
focus on books that foster Justice, Equality and
Sustainability. The Editor can be reached on
enquiries@palewellpress.co.uk

www.ingramcontent.com/pod-product-compliance
Lightning Source LLC
Chambersburg PA
CBHW060322030426
42336CB00011B/1159